Praise for Zachary Lazar's

EVENING'S EMPIRE

THE STORY OF MY FATHER'S MURDER

"*Evening's Empire*, which may be as close to watching a Scorsese film as one can get on the page, is infused with heat and action, jumpy snitches and crooked politicians and Chicago mobsters.... And yet Zachary Lazar also keeps it cool, playing the narrative much as Joan Didion does, the emotional withholding and near invisible release, as much happening between the lines as on them." —Nancy Rommelmann, *Portland Oregonian*

"One of the big themes of *Evening's Empire* is the writer's uneasy quest to understand how his father got mixed up in something criminal. Perhaps an even bigger question, additionally poignant because it is never quite articulated: Was the father a good guy or a bad guy?... The style is gorgeous—understated, precise, atmospheric. Like a pointillist painter, Lazar gives us vivid dots that are all the more powerful because we have to do the work of connecting them.... This is a personal story, and it's in the sections where the personal is acknowledged that *Evening's Empire* has its greatest power.... It's a spotty, murky, haunting story, told by a son who understands it better than his father ever could have."
  —Joan Wickersham, *Los Angeles Times*

"Zachary Lazar has managed an amazing feat—to evoke both Joan Didion's fierce intelligence and Truman Capote's eerie ability to enter into the unknown. And then there's the deep river of heartbreak flowing beneath it all. *Evening's Empire* is an incandescent masterpiece." —Nick Flynn, author of *Another Bullshit Night in Suck City* and *The Ticking Is the Bomb*

"'It was something out of a movie—not even a realistic movie,' reflects Zachary Lazar, struggling to reconstruct his father's inconceivable slide into scandal, corruption, and murder.... When irrefutable facts are few, the wise author resorts to atmosphere.... *Evening's Empire* is an artful exercise in reportorial chiaroscuro."
— Amanda Heller, *Boston Globe*

"Reading *Evening's Empire*, the story of a man who died without ever getting a clue about the world, you can't help but remember *Death of a Salesman*. 'Attention must be paid,' Willy Loman's anguished wife recited, and the same imperative applies here.... This little Arizona land scam was in some ways a mini-precursor of last year's subprime mortgage debacle. America never lacks for scoundrels or suckers, but which category did Zachary Lazar's father fall into? His son tries to find out here, in every kind of scholarly and journalistic way. It's terribly sad, this book. The author wants to honor his father, in the Old Testament sense of those words, but he's also bound by hard truth. He sees the pettiness, the futility. America, meet your pathetic hopes and dreams. Zachary, you've accomplished an amazing feat of filial piety."
—Caroline See, *Washington Post*

"Although *Evening's Empire* is categorized as both memoir and true crime, much of the book reads as a novel.... The multiplication of Warren's intrigues and a cumulative sense of doom supply its narrative drive."
—Laura Miller, Salon.com

"*Evening's Empire* is a brilliantly conceived, genre-bending story that features taut, exquisite prose about the murder of Zachary Lazar's father, via modes of the memoir, the novel, and investigative journalism."
—Chang-rae Lee, author of *Native Speaker* and *The Surrendered*

"Using interviews, research, and his ample storytelling gifts, Zachary Lazar guides us through the career of his father.... Like Lazar's novel *Sway*, the book has a heightened sense for the subtleties of influence and charisma, particularly Warren's.... Lazar can deliver scenes of criminal behavior that's at once deeply disturbing and morbidly comic.... *Evening's Empire* reveals a writer with emotional heft, terse prose, and searing insights into the complexities of a criminal world that must have looked pretty harmless— until it suddenly wasn't."   —Michael Miller, *Bookforum*

"Zachary Lazar deserves credit for doing something most children can't: look for the flaws in their parents after their death.... Using a handful of personal interviews and relying on extensive research from old newspapers and courtroom documents, Lazar creates a novel-like story about his father and the people involved. It's authentic, complete with real, noteworthy names... Joe Bonanno, Bruce Babbitt, and even Cesar Romero.... Reading it in 2009, there are elements that evoke scenes of the subprime lending market that helped balloon and eventually deflate America's real-estate industry."

—Mac Engel, *Dallas–Fort Worth Star-Telegram*

"Zachary Lazar channels Joan Didion in this unapologetically literary account of his father's murder."   —Tom Beer, *Newsday*

"Zachary Lazar has written a gripping book of unexpected beauty. In *Evening's Empire*, he remorselessly examines the ambiguous nature of both the shady deal and the good life. His analytic impulses soar with breathtaking imaginative leaps."

—Christopher Sorrentino, author of *Trance*,
a 2005 National Book Award finalist

"Fascinating.... A fantastic true crime tale, and a stunning follow-up to Lazar's *Sway*.... Lazar breaks down the late Edward Lazar's life, motivations, and mistakes in haunting, tragic detail. The result is part documentary, part narrative, a bold, immaculately planned study of what can go wrong in the quest for money, and the devastation of the American family.... Note the style—spare, direct, with a distinct lack of melodramatic flourish. This is as it should be. Lazar knows his father died brutally, and without mercy, and his text matches.... The book is his tribute to his father, and his opportunity to show the man that he does, indeed, hold him close to his heart."

—Christopher Schobert, *Buffalo News*

"'True crime' has such a florid, overdressed reputation that it pays to remember the genre's monuments—*In Cold Blood* or *The Executioner's Song*—are marked by their bloodless eloquence. Even the chronically feverish James Ellroy restrained himself in *My Dark Places*, a coolly deliberate autopsy of his mother's murder. It makes sense: for all the exhaustive research, interviews, and controlled dispassion, the identity of the real villain in these stories—profound personal loss—is known before you crack the covers. It's deprivation that breeds anger, and cosmic anger that runs these stories. The same can be said of Zachary Lazar's remarkable *Evening's Empire*.... It is a brave book, a project that promised to pay off its author in pain. What was Lazar going to discover about his dead father?... The disillusionment that fires his book, something Lazar knew was coming and that he went after anyway, manifests itself in a cold-burning anger. Lazar tries his best to control it, fails, and via his effort achieves a literary catharsis."

—John Anderson, *Newsday*

"An indelible portrait of the space-age suburbs and an American dream built on fraud." —Timothy Holder, *Details*

"*Evening's Empire* is a fascinating take on a time and a place, built from the inside out by a conspicuously interested party, as entertaining and evocative as could be, like a Scorsese movie, only richer, more thrilling for the memoir-like underpinnings. The story of Zachary Lazar's father is tricky and slippery, as mysterious as all those lights in the sky Arizona is so famous for, but much more human and down to earth. You'll want to put this one in the can't-put-it-down pile." —Frederick Barthelme, author of *Double Down* and *Waveland*

"Many men are murdered and, inevitably, some of them leave behind sons. But how many of those sons will turn out to be writers of economical but highly atmospheric prose?... Zachary Lazar has made the unusual, and admirable, choice to stay in the background." —Caroline Upcher, *East Hampton Star*

"*Evening's Empire* is a remarkable work of nonfiction in which reporting and imaginative empathy combine. Lazar's story of the murder of his father is spooky, sharply focused, loving, beautiful, and richly redolent of a recent America now vanished into the past." —Ian Frazier, author of *Family* and *Travels in Siberia*

EVENING'S EMPIRE

also by **ZACHARY LAZAR**

Sway

Aaron, Approximately

EVENING'S EMPIRE

THE STORY OF MY FATHER'S MURDER

ZACHARY LAZAR

BACK BAY BOOKS
Little, Brown and Company
NEW YORK   BOSTON   LONDON

Back Bay Books / Little, Brown and Company
Hachette Book Group
237 Park Avenue, New York, NY 10017
www.hachettebookgroup.com

Originally published in hardcover by Little, Brown and Company, November 2009
First Back Bay paperback edition, November 2010

Back Bay Books is an imprint of Little, Brown and Company. The Back Bay Books
name and logo are trademarks of Hachette Book Group, Inc.

The photographs on pages xiii, 116, and 199 are copyright © Bettmann / Corbis.

Author's note: The events in this book are based on my research of what
happened to my father over thirty years ago. Where the record was incomplete,
I have written what I think might have taken place.

Library of Congress Cataloging-in-Publication Data
Lazar, Zachary.
    Evening's empire : the story of my father's murder / Zachary Lazar.—1st ed.
    p. cm.
    ISBN 978-0-316-03768-6 (hc) / 978-0-316-03769-3 (pb)
    1. Lazar, Ed, d. 1975—Death and burial. 2. Lazar, Zachary—Family.
3. Murder—Arizona—Phoenix—Case studies. 4. Murder for hire—Arizona—
Phoenix—Case studies. 5. Accountants—Arizona—Phoenix—Biography.
6. Real property—Arizona—History—20th century. 7. Fraud—Arizona—
History—20th century. 8. Political corruption—Arizona—History—20th
century. 9. Organized crime—Illinois—Chicago—History—20th century.
10. Phoenix (Ariz.)—Biography. I. Title.
    HV6534.P55L394 2009
    364.152'3092—dc22   2009015512

10 9 8 7 6 5 4 3 2 1
RRD-IN

Book design by Fearn Cutler de Vicq
Printed in the United States of America

To my mother and Stacey and Richard

My God, my God, why hast thou forsaken me?
Why art thou so far from helping me; and from
The words of my roaring?

—**Psalm 22**

EVENING'S EMPIRE

PROLOGUE

In the fall of 1996, a few days after my wedding, an article about my father appeared in the *Arizona Republic*, an updating of the old, unhappy story:

> The men from Chicago were efficient.
>
> In the shadowy stairwell of the parking garage on North Central Avenue, they placed four .22-caliber shots into the chest of accountant Ed Lazar and one into the back of his head.
>
> They then partially unscrewed a light bulb near the door and disabled a fluorescent fixture, throwing the area into total darkness.
>
> It was hours before police found the body Feb. 19, 1975. It was two decades before they found out who killed Lazar and why.
>
> On Tuesday, they revealed the truth, along with information about a string of murders in Phoenix that they know or suspect was carried out by Chicago mob killers.
>
> That information, among other things,

3

throws new light on the murder of *Arizona Republic* reporter Don Bolles in 1976.

Phoenix police said that Ned Warren, Sr., then the king of Arizona land fraud, ordered the hit on Lazar, his bookkeeper and business partner.

They said John Harvey Adamson, the chief assassin in the Bolles killing, finally told police a year ago that Warren had ordered the hit on Lazar.

Adamson did not take part in the contract on Lazar, police said.

The killers who did take the contract, two Chicago Mafia hit men, murdered Lazar the day before he was to testify in front of a Maricopa County grand jury about Warren's bogus real-estate deals, in which millions of dollars were swindled from thousands of investors.

"He was going to name Ned Warren as the godfather of land fraud in Arizona," said Sgt. Mike Torres, a Phoenix police spokesman. "Ned Warren was the natural suspect, but there was no one to give him up."

Warren was eventually convicted of fraud and bribery and died in prison in 1980.

... "Ned Warren went to Adamson and asked him to kill three people; Lazar, (Arizona Real Estate Commissioner) J. Fred Talley and a third person whose name he could not remember," Torres said.

... Talley, who said he issued real-estate licenses to convicted felons, was suspended amid an investigation into whether he helped Warren in his activities.

Talley later retired and died of a heart attack.

> The new information about the Lazar kill-
> ing and the plan to kill Talley recalls a lurid
> period in Arizona's history—the late 1960s and
> 1970s—when land-fraud artists roamed the state
> in sharp suits, gouging money from buyers and
> investors across the country and the world.
>
> —*Arizona Republic,* October 2, 1996

Ninety miles north of Phoenix, in Yavapai County, Arizona, is a large subdivision of mobile homes and small, single-story houses called Verde Lakes. The land once belonged to a sprawling ranch, dating back to the late nineteenth century, when the nearby town of Camp Verde had been established to fend off raids from the Yavapai and Apache tribes that had lived for generations in that region. In the summer of 1969—the summer of the moon landing—my father, Edward Lazar, and his business partner, Ned Warren, Sr., financed a down payment on this land with a loan from a London-born entrepreneur named David Rich. They paid this money into a trust, and the company they formed, Consolidated Mortgage Corporation, hired crews to remake the ranch house into a clubhouse, to excavate a small lake where there had been none, to bring in breeding pairs of ducks, and to plant three-inch-high sapling trees. They did not build houses on the land, nor did they intend to. Verde Lakes existed as a possibility. As a fact, it was empty desert divided on a map into quarter-acre lots. The plan was to retail hundreds of these lots to small-scale inves-tors, many of them nearing retirement, who would build their own houses there or resell the land once its value rose. The company hired Cesar Romero, the actor most famous for playing the Joker on TV's *Batman*, as a public relations spokesman. They installed roads and utilities and water lines for homes that did not yet exist. They did all of this on credit, soliciting capital from banks, corporations, and private investors throughout the country, using as collateral and sometimes selling as securities the mortgages on the lots sold by the company's salesmen. For a brief while, my father was a paper millionaire. For a much longer time, he was in financial crisis. At one point, he and his partner, Warren, were personally $2 million in debt. When my father got out of the land business in 1973, he had nothing to show for his four years of struggle. I was five years old then. He was a devoted father according to everyone I've talked to, though I have almost no memories of him that I can feel certain are true and not the kind suggested by photographs.

On the *CBS Evening News* of February 21, 1975, Walter Cronkite appeared seated before a map of Arizona to deliver a story about my father and his business partner, Ned Warren, Sr. "Thousands of investors, many among those who could least afford it, have bought Arizona's land worth far less than they paid for it," Cronkite read. "The multimillion-dollar fraud is under investigation, but now there's a startling new development—a gangland-style murder."

Cronkite looked down at his cue card before reading the last phrase, as if the word *gangland*, pronounced by Cronkite as *ganglund*, could not be said without a slight pause to distance himself from its tabloid crudeness.

There was a shot of a stretcher being rolled toward an ambulance, an ambulance that to our eyes now looks like a large station wagon or a hearse. The body on the stretcher, covered with a blanket from foot to head, was identified by the on-scene reporter in the clipped style of a newsreel: "The victim, Edward Lazar, found in a Phoenix garage Wednesday with five bullets in his body."

The two homicide detectives in their sport coats collapsed the stretcher and pushed it into the ambulance. There was an image now of a press photo of my father's face. The cameramen had positioned the photo on a bed of fabric so that, with this border, the picture could fit the dimensions of a TV screen. It was black and white—all of this footage was in black and white. When you watch it now, it has the unreal quality of a crime movie trying to capture a "period."

My father looked eager and shrewd in the photograph. He was still in his early thirties when it was taken. His eyes penetrated the frame, as if he could easily and accurately read the gaze of whoever might be looking back at him. His dark hair was short and his lips were parted, not in a smile, but as if to say something precise and illuminating in the midst of a dispute.

The reporter continued: "Lazar was scheduled to appear yesterday before a grand jury investigating sales of virtually worthless land for as much as four hundred million dollars. Lazar's testimony was expected to focus on his onetime business associate, Ned Warren, Sr., a mysterious figure widely known in Arizona as 'the Godfather of Land Fraud.'"

That phrase, "the Godfather of Land Fraud," had bedeviled my father for at least five months before his death, since Warren's first indictment. It had started as a joke—two or three years before, someone had given Warren a birthday present of director's chairs printed with the words *The Godfather* on the backs—but now the joke had become an epithet in dozens of newspaper stories written about Warren, often containing a reference to his prison record, his land "swindles," and, most recently, the payments that he, along with my father and other associates, had made to government officials. The word *Godfather* now chimed with the word *gangland* to produce *Mafia*.

On-screen, the handsome, sixty-year-old Warren moved slowly and confidently down a courthouse hallway, trailed by reporters and cameramen. He was faintly smiling, well dressed in a conservative gray suit, his hands either crossed in front of his waist or in the pockets of his pants. He looked as if the extent of his secrets was faintly comic to him, as if no one would ever suspect half the things he knew, or as if most of what he had done would be impossible to prove. He seemed to know all of this as he walked the courthouse hallway, and he wasn't wrong.

I have an essay my father wrote when he was twelve years old, a schoolboy's essay about the Hebrew poet Hayim Bialik. In 1946, the essay won first prize ("Choice of $25 U.S. Savings Bond or a week at Herzl Camp") in an annual contest held by the Minneapolis Zionist Youth Commission.

> ...Bialik's popularity should not only be attributed to his poetic genius, but also to his personality in general, to his brilliancy of thought and to his responsoveness [sic] to the needs of his people.
>
> As long as there lives a Jew who still delights in beauty, imagery, and poetry, so long will the immortal words of Hayim Nachman Bialik be found on the lips, in the minds and in the hearts of Israel.

When I first discovered this essay, I saw in it evidence of a straight-A student, earnest, eager to please. When I looked at it a little longer, I saw evidence of a boy smart enough to conceal a total lack of interest in the poems of Hayim Bialik beneath a lilting arrangement of phrases ("on the lips, in the minds and in the hearts of Israel"). I don't know how to connect the fact that my father saved this essay and prize citation with the fact that he was murdered in a garage. His story refutes an idea I seem still incapable of outgrowing, the idea that who we are plays some part in shaping our lives, or, as Heraclitus put it, that character is fate.

Five bullets. One in the back of my father's head, four in his chest. At nine o'clock in the morning on February 19, my father, arriving at work in an office building on Phoenix's North Central Avenue, was met by two hit men from Chicago, Lee DiFranco* and Robert Hardin, who forced him into a stairwell and shot him five times with a .22 semiautomatic pistol fitted with a homemade silencer, probably a Coke bottle. They left the shell casings on the ground but unscrewed the fluorescent light in the stairwell to prevent anyone from discovering too soon what they'd done. After taking whatever cash had been in my father's money clip, DiFranco, according to Hardin's account, placed a dime on my father's forehead. They left behind his car keys and credit cards, and they left his briefcase on the ground outside the opened door of his Pontiac Grand Ville. They were paid $10,000 for this. Neither of them ever went to jail.

---

* DiFranco's name has been changed.

. . .

Ned Warren didn't speak on the CBS Evening News of February 21. He was "not available to newsmen," the reporter said.

Instead, the next person to speak was Attorney General Bruce Babbitt, future candidate for president, future secretary of the interior, at that moment riding the land fraud scandals in Arizona toward the state's governorship. In 1975, he was gangly and wore glasses, and he hunched forward in his chair like a graduate student in a seminar room. "As a prosecutor," he said, clearing his throat, "I'm not about to speculate publicly about who murdered Ed Lazar. But when a man with Lazar's knowledge and background is murdered on his way to the grand jury, in the style in which he was murdered, it would be very coincidental to attribute it to some extraneous reason that is not related to those facts."

The last man to speak put it more bluntly. He was another of Warren's former business associates, a man named James Cornwall. He was tall and slightly jowly, with the sideburns and pomaded hair of the revivalist preacher Billy Graham—appropriate, since Cornwall had just become a minister himself. His suit and tie were of an expensive-looking subtle plaid, and he sat with one hand across his knee to reveal an elegant wristwatch. He seemed at ease, despite the fact that he was facing sixty-six counts of fraud, forty years in prison.

"Mr. Warren has told me he had the ability to pick up the phone and have people maimed or killed," Cornwall said. "I believed it at the time, and I believe it now."

On the afternoon before this story appeared on the CBS Evening News, more than four hundred people had attended my father's memorial service at the Sinai Mortuary Chapel, which did not have enough seats for such a large crowd. There were my parents' friends—the Korts and the Goodmans, the Finebergs and the Starrs, the Kobeys and the Shers—young Jewish couples, their children in school for the day. There were our next-door neighbors, Carol and Dick Nichols, who had taken me the night before with their sons, David and Craig, to a soapbox derby and spaghetti dinner to give me some time away from the confusion of adults crowding our house. There were members of the Jewish Community Center, where my parents played tennis, and of Temple Beth Israel, where my sister, Stacey, and I went to the annual Purim carnivals dressed in costumes my mother made out of towels, construction paper, and glitter. There were my grandparents on both sides, my aunts and uncles. There were the associates of Gallant, Farrow, and of Laventhol, Krekstein, Horwath and Horwath, the accounting firms my father had worked for before and after his stint in the land business. David Rich, the London-born entrepreneur, was there. Ned Warren, though he had befriended my parents socially in the four years my father was his business partner, was not.

None of it made any sense to the people at the memorial service—this story of hit men in a stairwell, Ned Warren picking up a phone and ordering them there. It was something out of a movie—not even a realistic movie. There was the grief over the young man they'd all had a special liking for, and then there was the sense that his death would never seem real, that the sudden violence was so incongruous with his personality that the two could not be held in the mind at the same time. They thought about my father's sly smile, the way he sometimes seemed to look at everybody from an amused distance, and then they thought about the front-page photo of his body slumped in a stairwell, the banner headline: *Grand Jury Witness in Probe of Warren Is Slain Gang Style*. His friends were in the furniture business or in real estate, practiced law or accounting or engineering. Their wives played mah-jongg and tennis and golf. Like my father, the men rooted for the ASU football team, took their families on vacation to Lake Havasu or San Diego. My father could be quiet. There was something he held in reserve, a mystery about him, even a romance, but there wasn't crookedness, there wasn't criminality. He was not your average CPA—women liked him, he had an adventurous side, he liked to drink. This adventurous side may have been why he got into a risky business like land development in the first place. But no one at the memorial service imagined he had "ties to the underworld," or even knowledge of enough wrongdoing to be murdered. No one thought that.

In the parking lot outside, a reporter named Al Sitter from the *Arizona Republic* was taking down license plate numbers to see if any of them corresponded to figures of organized crime. The shame, added to the grief, was now beginning. Before long, my father would be appearing in news stories as the "lieutenant" to Ned Warren's "Godfather," the one man, now dead, who had "intimate knowledge" of the full extent of Warren's criminality. Eventually, my father would come to look like a con man with a flashy suit and a Cadillac, or even a full-blown mobster, perhaps a relative of the Jewish gangster Hymie Lazar, as one line of thought ran. He was murdered twice in this way.

I remember his forehead being broad, with lines scored across it (lines that even then I thought I would inherit and by doing so know I was an adult). I used to try on his boots, stumbling toward the fireplace, with its mesh screen pulled closed by a thin chain. I remember the family room's white shag rug, its console stereo with the plastic arm on which you could stack several records at once. I remember an avocado linoleum floor in the kitchen, a "passway" that looked into the living room (dark in memory, small and long). The living room, the family room, the kitchen—I remember the rooms. Whatever I write here about my father will have to be a kind of conjuration.

The evening the two detectives came to our door to bring us the news of the murder, my mother sent my sister and me to our rooms. From across the house, I could hear my mother laughing, a high-pitched, unabashed kind of laughter that sounded more and more illicit as it went on. When I went out to see what was happening, she was sitting on the couch, bowing and rising like a marionette, or as though someone was shoving her from behind, only to yank her back upright with her blouse in his fist. When she looked at me, she screamed, her face distorted. The scream was angry, personal, insane.

Almost from that moment, we stopped talking about it. As time passed, there were fewer and fewer occasions on which it made sense to try. To do so was to return on some level to my mother screaming in the living room.

I have always had two ideas: that one day I would have to write about my father's story, and that if I ever did so I would never be able to write another thing again. What story could compare with his? The question was a more specific case of a larger dilemma: What could I ever do that would not seem trivial compared with what he went through?

The author (right) and his friend and
next-door neighbor David Nichols

It took me ten years to start. In the ten years I waited, some people who might have told me things died. When I at last flew to Phoenix, a week before Christmas 2006, I wasn't thinking very much about what I was doing. I had put the trip together in such a hasty way that I had no time to consider my expectations. The pilot announced we were beginning our descent toward Sky Harbor Airport, and I was there. I had a stack of newspaper clippings, a few relevant books, the addresses of the people and places I was going to visit. I had appointments and dinners set up for every night I would be there. I would wake up at six-thirty every morning and go to bed at midnight, and every moment of that time I would be following a schedule, not thinking about it.

He was "not a big talker"—this was something I had learned from my interviews over the phone with some of my father's friends. He "could keep a secret," one of them said, "as you know." My father's onetime roommate Barry Starr had lived in the same apartment with him for three years and still felt he never knew him, that he remained a mystery. Phone calls would sometimes come to the apartment from a woman named Ruth, a woman who was otherwise a total secret. Only years later did Barry Starr learn that Ruth was Ed's ex-wife, that they had a son together named Richard.

The story is not in one anecdote or newspaper article, but in two hundred anecdotes and newspaper articles. The story is in the relationship between eight thousand facts that for weeks and months seemed to have no relationship at all.

A young accountant takes a chance: he goes into business with a man who has "a not very savory reputation," a man who in fact has a criminal record. No one knows exactly why he does this. This is the first mystery. It has something to do with his having a secretive side: he "could almost lead two lives," according to one friend. It has something to do with his being adventurous, with his not being your average CPA.

A kind of conjuration. You look at the facts and see an intricate puzzle with some pieces missing. You establish a time line. You think of possible motives, of psychology. You piece together what you know and imagine how things could have played out in rooms forty years ago, most of the players long since dead.

PAGE TWO PX 183 94 EX T 0

ANGELES PD ADVISED ON [   ] AT [   ] LAS VEGAS

SUBJECT ANTHONY JOHN SPILOTRO, FBI NUMBER 860 L42B HAD BEEN

OBSERVED WITH LOS ANGELES SUBJECT [   ] FBI

NUMBER [   ] AT STAK'S RESTAURANT, 5223 WEST CENTURY BOULEVARD,

ENGLEWOOD, CALIFORNIA. SPILOTRO AND [   ] ARE [   ]

OF [   ], FBI NUMBER [   ] WHO IS UNDER

INVESTIGATION AT LOS ANGELES IN CAPTIONED MATTER. LOS ANGELES PD

INDICATED SPILOTRO AND [   ] WERE OBSERVED MEETING WITH AN

UNIDENTIFIED MALE AND FEMALE WHO OPERATED A 1973 WHITE OVER MAROON

OLDSMOBILE BEARING ARIZONA LICENSE [   ] LISTED TO [   ]

[   ] PHOENIX, ARIZONA. LOS

ANGELES AND PHOENIX INDICES NEGATIVE RE [   ]. THE UNKNOWN

SUBJECTS WERE FOLLOWED BY LOS ANGELES PD OFFICERS SOUTH ON

INTERSTATE 605 TOWARD SAN DIEGO AND CONTACT WITH AUTOMOBILE DROPPED

IN VICINITY OF FOUNTAIN VALLEY, CALIFORNIA.

    UNKNOWN SUBJECTS DESCRIBED AS WHITE MALE, [   ] YEARS, [   ] FEET [   ]

INCHES, [   ] POUNDS, MOD STYLE, [   ] HAIR, [   ]

[   ] WEARING [   ] JACKET WITH [   ] TROUSERS. WHITE

FEMALE, [   ] YEARS, [   ] FEET [   ] INCHES, [   ] POUNDS, [   ].

b6
b7C

A typical page from the FBI file on the author's father

PART ONE

Asked how his son became involved with Warren, Louis Lazar replied:

"Some fellows were making pretty good money in the land development business. Ed was a very bright young man. He saw other fellows making money and thought he should have a good land development business also. And he did have it for awhile."

Ervin Berman, 7430 E. Chaparral, Edward Lazar's father-in-law, said the murder victim never discussed his business dealings with him.

"Ed wasn't much of a talker and, of course, we never pushed it," Berman said. "We didn't know what was going on and we hoped it would just be forgotten."

—*Arizona Republic*, February 21, 1975

I

It was tax season, March 1959, but Ed was not in the office, as he might have been even on a Sunday evening that time of year. He was on the basketball court of a public high school, shooting baskets with some teenage boys. He'd been in Phoenix for almost a year now but still wasn't used to a March evening being 70 degrees. The sky was striated with thin, twisting clouds the color of salmon. Everything was dry, and he could breathe easily. He had left his parents and brother in Minneapolis to come to Phoenix in part because he had asthma. Basketball was good for quieting his mind, something about the rhythm of it, the repetition of an easy task—shooting a basket—that eight or nine times out of ten went right. What was on his mind was not taxes, but his girlfriend back in Minnesota, Ruth, who had just called him again long-distance. It weighed on him like a dream in which dark images—snakes, blood, weeds—asserted themselves as more real than the furniture and clothing of everyday life. Ruth was not Jewish; his parents did not approve of her. As for the child she was pregnant with, it was something he couldn't even mention to his parents, nor was the baby quite real to him—not a child that he would one day love, but a problem he didn't know how to solve. He was twenty-six, had never been responsible for anyone in his life, had never set foot into the arena of seriousness. On the basketball court, he was still Eddie, a successful young CPA who was amused by how it looked to be shooting baskets with a bunch of teenagers.

A rebound came high off the rim toward him and he put up a set shot that bounced off the backboard and through the net. The boys dribbled and looked at him, then went back to the respectful, silent appraisal of two different basketballs in motion, the alternation of shots. Ed missed from outside. He stepped forward for a rebound, allowing his momentum to carry him up the key, dribbling twice, then striding into the air for a layup. He was the quiet instigator of his group of bachelor friends, someone who was always near the action but who never tripped up, never got caught. He and his buddies drove to Pasadena for the Rose Bowl. They went to Nogales, Mexico, for Cinco de Mayo, where two years ago they saw the greatest living bullfighter, Carlos Aruza. The small guard driving the lane had to move to the basket and just assume that the path would somehow clear up, that by leaping into a crowd of defenders he would manage to get by them, that they would fall away.

A quick marriage in Minneapolis, the birth of a son, then, just as quickly, the marriage over, the father gone, the mother and son left behind in Minnesota.

People always talked about Eddie's smile, his devious, quiet smile. You didn't get it constantly, so it never seemed like something he used on purpose. It seemed spontaneous and slightly wicked, irresistible. A year later, Ruth moved to Phoenix to be near him so that their son, Richard, could be near him. She asked him for nothing he didn't want to give. Life went back to normal—easy, a report card full of As. He was smart and optimistic, not a person who imagined himself being duped or tricked in any way.

Men wore cowboy hats in Phoenix. They wore bolo ties, braided leather cords with clasps, like a silver coin or a silver steer's head. Some of them spoke with western accents and had the gruff faces of Dust Bowl farmers. Others might wear a western vamp on their suit jackets, but when they spoke you heard Pittsburgh or Detroit. He noticed that there were a surprising number of Jews in the city, and in fact the power structure contained many Jews, although they were different from the Jews of the East Coast or even the Midwest. Like the half-Jewish Barry Goldwater, some of them looked, acted, and talked like ranchers or citrus growers, conversant with irrigation, railroads, military bases, oil. Ed often felt as if he were on the set of a movie that didn't quite make sense. He played tennis and a little golf. He ate Mexican food. He still dressed like a member of Sigma Alpha Mu: madras blazers with thin lapels, loafers, oxford-cloth shirts with button-down collars. In Phoenix, it was the costume of the Bright Young Man, the new pool of college-educated businessmen, lawyers, and accountants who, along with the retirees, had helped triple the city's population in the last decade. The land boom was just starting, and if you were an accountant in Phoenix, you had a clear view of all the money suddenly sprouting up out of nothing—not out of cotton farming or citrus orchards but out of simple land, empty land fed by the dams and canals of the Salt River Project, the Verde River Project. There was the state's year-round sunshine. There was the newly affordable luxury of air conditioning. There was expanded air travel, and there were new highways, cheap gasoline, an understanding that you could leave a place like Minneapolis, Minnesota, without severing all ties to your past.

On New Year's Day 1960, a hundred thousand people—ten times more than expected—arrived from all over the United States to attend the grand opening of Sun City, a development for retired people on Phoenix's northwestern edge. It seemed to appear instantaneously, a self-contained world. Enriched by the building of Las Vegas casinos, the Del Webb Corporation had spent $2.5 million erecting model homes in five different styles, planting mature palms along newly paved streets, installing shopping and recreation centers, establishing a golf course on what had been bare desert. In the first year, the Del Webb Corporation sold almost fifteen hundred houses. The sales brought in $17.5 million.

Fifteen million dollars gross in the first year. It made the cover of *Time* magazine. All over the country, people of a certain cast of mind were coming to understand that Arizona had a lot of empty land.

He was an accountant, not a businessman. He could add up a page-long column of seven-digit numbers by running the tip of a pencil down the ledger like a pointer, figuring in his head, never using a calculator. He did it with the stern expression of a surgeon making an incision. He approached his job seriously, more seriously than many people approached their jobs, but as with many men his mind was a system of switches, and in different settings he was a different person. In college, at the University of Minnesota, his favorite professor had thought that businessmen were "shills," "daredevils," while accountants were problem solvers, ensuring that each quarter the businessman and his company booked more earnings than they paid out in tax. Ed had believed this in college. He had believed that the best thing in the world to be was smart, as opposed to a "daredevil." It took him longer than it took many people to realize how obviously untrue this was. He began to sense people moving forward, leaving him behind—people in real estate, people in medicine, even people with restaurants. By his early thirties, he had begun to wonder how he had ended up preparing tax strategies and financial statements for people so much less intelligent than he was.

"You need to sharpen your pencil," he told his son Richie, as soon as Richie was old enough to write or even draw. "You can't work with that pencil. There's no point in sitting down to work with a pencil like that."

He didn't recognize himself in Ruth's apartment. If he had watched a film of himself lecturing Richie, he wouldn't have understood his tone and would have been surprised to see the scene play itself out as it did. It did not jibe with the Ed Lazar who drove every Saturday to Tempe to see the Sun Devils game, or who traded the same birthday card every year with his friend Ron Fineberg, his drinking buddy, who, like the birthday card, was the same age year after year.

Miss Susan Berman became the bride of Edward Lazar during an early evening ceremony in Congregation Keneseth Israel. After a reception, the pair departed for a honeymoon in California. A Valley residence is planned.

For her vows, the bride chose a floor-length

sheath styled with an empire waistline and dotted with pearl applique. The ensemble was accented by a lace mantilla.

—*Arizona Republic*, August 24, 1965

She had given Ed Lazar an ultimatum. Her job would end in June—she was a speech therapist in the public schools—and if he didn't ask her to marry him, she would go back to her home in Elgin, Illinois.

It was time to grow up—he knew it himself. She hadn't had to put it that way.

Her name was Susan, but everyone called her Susie. She looked like a young Elizabeth Taylor, with high cheekbones that set off her green eyes. One day his father, who had moved down to Phoenix from Minneapolis, had seen her sitting in the waiting room of a dentist's office and got her phone number and address from the receptionist. That was how they had met—the right girl this time, a Jewish girl from a small town in Illinois.

They would discover mysterious or unspoken things about each other in the next months and years, starting with Ed's past—a son named Richie, an ex-wife named Ruth. He had been anxious about telling her, and yet it hadn't mattered to her, his past. She had already fallen in love, had already made up her mind to marry him by the time he'd told her those things. He was not your average CPA. That was part of the attraction, and also the source of some restlessness in him that she didn't understand, the source of an ongoing tension that would arise between them. Once they were married, there were his late nights in bars, Tuesdays or Thursdays, weeknights. She knew there were reasons men went to bars and one of those reasons was conversation with male friends, and she also knew there were other reasons. They worked things out, used humor to bring themselves back to each other. They went to Sedona, San Diego, the Peach Bowl in Atlanta. They had beautiful parties at their house, festive picnics at Encanto Park. They had two children. They loved each other most in the last year of their marriage, after near-bankruptcy had taught them to appreciate what they had in a new way. They had nine years, five months, and twenty-seven days to try to find out who the other really was.

"A Valley residence is planned." The author's childhood home.

2

There were many Ned Warrens. There was the blunt "N. J. Warren" that appeared on the business stationery, the more personable "Ned" who shook your hand and asked what you'd like to drink. There were the variations "Nathan Warren," "Nathan J. Warren," and "Nathan Jacques Warren" that appeared on his police record, which, when he first came to Phoenix, nobody had seen. There was the birth name, "Nathan Jacques Waxman," which in its Jewish fussiness simply didn't have the trustworthy, red-blooded ring of "Ned Warren, Sr."

In November 1961, two days after arriving in Phoenix, he walked through the carport of a rental house with a newspaper and a paper sack containing milk, bacon, eggs. His wife, Barbara, was already serving toast with butter and sugar to the children. He put his cigarette out in an ashtray on the kitchen counter, said nothing, placed the eggs and bacon and milk in the refrigerator, shutting it no harder than necessary and in this way expressing his detachment from the scene.

"You beat me to it," he said over his shoulder.

"The kids were starving," said Barbara.

"Wouldn't want anyone to starve. Not on a school day."

He went through the low-ceilinged passage into the dim hallway with its brown carpeting, unfolding the newspaper in his hands. For a moment, after the bright sunlight outside and the bright lights of the kitchen, he was almost blind, and he had to look down at his feet to steady himself as he walked. Donna Stevens was in the second bedroom down, standing in a frayed black slip among the opened cardboard boxes, smoking a cigarette. She and Barbara were almost exactly the same age, former roommates.

"Douglas MacArthur's *Reminiscences,*" she said, covering her breast with her hand. "You're going to give those as gifts."

"Not everyone drinks," said Warren. "Some people like to read."

"Some people have a pulse."

The room was littered with papers—stationery, ad samples, résumés, letters—and boxes of odds and ends—books, bottles of Scotch and liqueur, packaged nuts. They had all driven in a convoy from Florida—Donna, Barbara, and Warren in separate cars—and in the two days since their arrival they had only started to unpack.

"I thought I'd call Roeder's office around ten o'clock," Donna said, straightening at Warren's touch. " 'Mr. Warren will be free anytime between noon and two-thirty. He's very much looking forward to meeting the senator, can he stop by—' "

"I already spoke to John Roeder," Warren said, turning away. "Last night, we spoke. We're old pals now. You can call if you want, but I'll just drop in."

He leaned on a stack of boxes, leafing through the classifieds section of the paper, looking for his ad. It said, under the words *Advertising . . . Insurance . . . Real Estate . . . Land:*

I Can Sell Anything.

He had, as he would tell it later, "three cars, two women, three kids, a dog, a cat, and eight hundred dollars." His mother, now living in New York, had given him the name of a state senator, John Roeder, the son of a friend, and that was all he had to go on for now. But it was part of a cycle he'd been through many times already. He was forty-six and had already had many lives, many incarnations.

I Can Sell Anything.

He got a job selling undeveloped land outside Wickiup, in Mohave County, for a man named George Wickman at the Star Development Corporation. When they disagreed over sales practices, he got a job with Richard Frost at the Arizona Land Corporation, or ALCO. He used the reference from John Roeder for both jobs. From his car, he'd viewed the respective subdivisions—not the spectacular pink rock of the Grand Canyon, nor the Phoenix Valley, with its eerie ranks of saguaro rising on the mountainsides like abstracted human figures. The subdivisions were fenced off by rusted lengths of barbed wire. There was nothing to see but clumps of gray rock and sand, a dry bush here and there—cholla, ocotillo. You looked out the car window at it and you felt abandoned, futile. The nearest town had a gas station and the ruined barracks of a government boarding school where Apache children, taken from their homes, had been made to speak English.

Thirty dollars an acre—sometimes less—retailed at whatever markup you dared to ask. There was something solid and immutable about the land that felt like a counterweight to all human foolishness. You cut it up into squares and laced barbed wire around the edges and the land did nothing, as if it knew that you and the barbed wire would go away. Its value was not just symbolic. It was not just gold, it was earth. You could call it "North Star Hills," create a logo and a slogan, print fliers with an artist's rendition of the golf course and trout pond planned for next year, and the barrenness of the land would seem to justify your deceit, for the barrenness was eternal.

He had a criminal record, so he could not get a license to sell real estate in Arizona. When Richard Frost found out he'd been working without a license, he was fired again, but three days later he formed two corporations, Grace and Co. and Diamond Valley, so that he could carry on as a broker for Frost's ALCO without the name "Ned Warren" appearing on its payroll. Richard Frost kept his ties to Warren because Warren could sell anything, including isolated, quarter-acre parcels of desert scrub. It didn't matter if the buyers could even afford the payments on their lots. What mattered in the land business, as Warren saw immediately, was not the sale of land but the generation of contracts and mortgages, indebitures that could be sold to a third party—a bank or an investor—or used as collateral for a loan—abstraction upon abstraction, world without end.

The term for the mortgages was *paper*. A bundle of mortgages was called a *package*. There was nothing illegal about selling paper to a third party. There was nothing illegal about paying $25 to set up a corporation with your mistress, Donna Stevens, as president, and yourself, the sole stockholder, unlisted as a company officer. It was simply a way to make money, a way a person with $800 and a criminal record could have a chance at becoming a millionaire.

Making no little plans, Phoenix' movers and shakers count on atomic energy to provide some day the vast power needed to bring salty Pacific seawater fresh into the desert.

—*Time*, February 15, 1960

It came out when Warren was still in prison, a four-page story in *Time* magazine about the economic boom in Phoenix. It described a spendthrift city of Cadillacs and golf courses and fashion boutiques in adjacent Scottsdale. It told of a cocktail party at which, on the spur of the moment, a group of drinkers had put together almost $1 million to create a new building downtown, the Guaranty Bank Building. Drinkers, fantasists—the money in Phoenix looked childlike, something out of a Hollywood farce. But all his life he had banked on the Hollywood farce. Only the naive thought that the Hollywood farce was not an accurate reflection of the way things worked.

In the *Time* article, there was a profile of a young millionaire named Lee Ackerman, a land developer who was planning a run for governor that year. When Warren first met Ackerman, it was the fall of 1963, almost four years after the article in *Time*. They were in a room full of businessmen and their wives, gathered there to raise funds for Warren's acquaintance, Ackerman's friend, John Roeder, the state senator. Ackerman was a member of the Democratic National Committee. He had been a hero in World War II, a pilot in Africa. People in Phoenix thought of him the way they thought of JFK.

"I see you were talking to my friend Dave Rich over there," Ackerman said, shaking Warren's hand.

"Dave Rich from London," Warren said.

"A character. He couldn't believe the sun when he first came here. London was still a ruin then—there was still rubble from the war. He came here on vacation and he never went back. He and I went in on some land deals and he made so much money that I sold him my summerhouse in San Diego."

Warren nodded. *He and I*—the good grammar struck him. "I'm in the land business also," he said. "Mostly north of here, in Navajo County. We should get together sometime for a drink."

The story of David Rich was a token, he realized, a cliché about the American dream that even Ackerman knew was corny, but it was the kind of cliché that everyone agreed with, that opened the door for relationships. He guessed what Ackerman was thinking: that Warren had arrived in Phoenix with a stake raised back East in machinery or electronics. He looked at Ackerman and saw a displaced Harvard graduate—he remembered Harvard from the *Time* article—still buying clothes from Brooks Brothers, a winning figure made lazy by a lack of competitors. Warren wore a gray suit and a dark tie and a no-nonsense silver wristwatch. He had the trim body of an athlete. He liked Ackerman immediately—they liked each other immediately. They talked about Cambridge and Boston, where Warren happened to have grown up—the Lawrence School, Worcester Academy, not Harvard in Warren's case, but Penn. When Ackerman mentioned he was from St. Louis, Warren responded genially, not with the Cardinals but with talk about the Italian restaurants on The Hill—not with the obvious but with the specific. He showed Ackerman a picture of a Rolls-Royce he'd looked at on a recent trip to London, speaking of London. "Too expensive, but a beauty," he said. He confided in Ackerman about the back pain he sometimes got, and Ackerman liked him for the comic way he bent over and rubbed his spine, his drink rattling in the other hand. He didn't seem to be the kind of person who would ever get back pain.

He saw the openings before other people did. He saw them and exploited them, not for the money—not entirely, or even primarily—but because the game fascinated him, its secrecy and complications. It was not money, it was the feeling of invisibility, of walking into a room and finding the weak points, working your way through the scenarios, thinking three steps ahead, effacing your own cunning so that nobody but you would ever have the chance to admire it.

"I want you and the others to go over to the bars on Van Buren tomorrow night," he told Tony Serra, a lot salesman at ALCO with skeptical, sleepy eyes. "Not a fancy bar, go to Van Buren, or the Ivanhoe, the dives. Offer everybody a hundred dollars, give them a name, get them to sign the name on a contract. Not 'John Doe.' Not 'Joe Smith.' Use a good name. Get the phone book and find some real names."

Serra looked down, drawing some lines on a notepad on his thigh. "A pretty easy sell," he said. "The Ivanhoe on a Friday night."

"Make sure the address is a real address, the name is a real name. You've filled out enough credit reports by now to know how this is done."

The contracts he gave Serra were ALCO contracts, but the land was not ALCO's land. In a way, it was nobody's land. It was state land, mostly uninhabitable, a few compass points on a surveyor's map.

"What if someone actually calls the phone numbers on those sales?" Serra said.

"They're not going to call the phone numbers. They're going to call the Diamond Valley Corporation if they ever have a problem, but they're not going to have a problem."

"They're not going to get paid."

"They're going to get paid. Why wouldn't they get paid?"

Serra thought about it for a moment. In St. Louis, he had been in the insurance business for a while, another commission-based business, so he knew a little bit about how this was done: sell the policy, split the commission with the buyer, make a few payments to quell suspicion, then let the policy lapse. "You're going to make the payments yourself," he said.

"Someone's going to buy a mortgage from me for thirty-five hundred dollars," Warren said. "ALCO's going to pay me a seven-hundred-dollar commission for making this sale. It doesn't cost me very much to keep up the payments for a few months to make it look right. I've already made forty-two hundred dollars."

Serra nodded. "Poor Dick Frost."

"You're not bad. You see where this is going."

"I guess, what, eventually you assign them one of Dick's mortgages. Switch it out for a good one. Give Dick the delinquents."

"Something like that. I may run it through a few corporations first, to make it more complicated. There's a lot of different ways."

No buyer, no land. Out of nowhere, a $3,500 mortgage with an address and a phone number and a credit history. The buyer and the land were ciphers anyway. No one ever came to see their lots—their lots were too far away to go and see. It would be years before they had enough equity to claim title to their lots. They put 10 percent down, signed a mortgage for the rest, and you sold the mortgage for cash. There was no real reason not to sell the same lot over and over again—no one ever owned it or even knew if it was there. It got him thinking about the possibility of using no land at all.

Dear _____,

It has come to our attention that the purchaser of lot X in the Arizona Land Corporation subdivision Y is no longer current with payments on mortgage Z, as administered for us by the Minnesota Title Company. As per our contractual agreement, Diamond Valley

> *Corp. is hereby reassigning you Arizona Land Corpo-*
> *ration mortgage A on lot B in the same subdivision,*
> *of equivalent value. Your monthly disbursement will*
> *remain the same. We hope that our prompt attention*
> *to this matter will inspire your continued confidence*
> *in your investment program with Diamond Valley.*

Insects, creosote, mesquite. Dry land under sunlight, dry land under darkness—the silence of rocks, the silence of sand in wind, the dark sky, the stars. The stillness of scrubland, dry washes, box canyons, gulches. The barbed wire sagging and rusting on posts.

Before you could even put in a road or a water line, you first had to find investors to buy the land as it was. Or if you could not find them, you could invent them. No need then for the slide presentation to a room full of sixty-year-olds in a hotel restaurant in Buffalo. No need for the boiler room, the ten salesmen claiming that the Gallo Wine Company was moving three thousand jobs to Navajo County and land prices were about to soar.

Build up a company on paper, inflating its value with a flood of sales, a flood of cash flow. After compromising its assets, taking as much as you could, sell the company to someone else. He would find, over time, that the process usually took about eighteen months. He sold Lee Ackerman Diamond Valley in early 1965, more or less on this schedule.

They went to the police department on Washington Street—business partners now—to register Warren as an out-of-state convict. This was on February 18, 1965. Afterward, Ackerman drove Warren uptown to North 44th Street to speak to the real estate commissioner, J. Fred Talley, about finally getting a license.

In his briefcase, Warren had an envelope containing $200, a measly figure he had picked himself, but having seen Talley a few times before, he knew he had not underestimated him.

He had "spent some time with Uncle Sam," he'd told Ackerman, implying that it was for tax evasion, something that could have happened to anyone with the wrong accountant. "Lots of hassles and lots of ways around the hassles—that's what my year in Danbury was like. Probably not so different from the air force," he'd said. It somehow sealed their relationship, the casual way he spoke of his time in prison. Ackerman happened to belong to a group called Heart, Inc., which helped find employment for rehabilitated convicts. Warren's past made him feel like a friend, not just a business partner. His rehabilitation was an indication of things they had in common: resilience, grit, an instinct that the world was manageable if you had half a brain.

"This is Uncle Fred," Ackerman said, standing behind the commissioner, leaning forward with his hands on Talley's shoulders. "Uncle Fred is a tough old sumbuck."

Talley was still seated at his desk, looking dyspeptically at Warren with small eyes behind large, dark-framed glasses. He was a fat man with a sunken chin and protruding ears and a pinched, inverted mouth—a slumping octopus of a man in a brown suit and a bolo tie.

"Nice to see you, Fred," said Warren drily.

"Don't get me all greased up. It's too early in the day to get fucked," Talley said.

"All this barnyard talk. I'm not used to it."

Talley put a fist to his mouth and coughed. "Lee's an old friend of mine," he said. "That's why you're here. You know how many people I have working under me?"

"I have no idea."

"Three. Three investigators for the state of Arizona. All I can do is make your life a little harder or easier. Just like you can make mine harder or easier."

Ackerman patted Talley's shoulders and indicated that Warren should sit down in one of the chairs in front of the commissioner's desk. "I hear you got top scores on the exam," Ackerman said, looking at Warren.

Warren didn't answer. He saw that Talley had the license already prepared, saw it sitting on top of a pile of documents. Talley slid it across his desk and Warren looked at the commissioner's signature and the state seal and then at his own name, *Nathan J. Warren*, typed in beside the words *Western Growth Capital, Inc.*, the name of the land company he had just started with Ackerman after selling him Diamond Valley.

"Tell your son he can start work next month," Warren said to Talley.

"Give him till May. Let's say May fifteenth."

"Fine. I've got something for you in a little envelope here."

"Tell your friend John Roeder it's been a long time."

"I'll do that. I'm sure we'll all be seeing a lot of each other from now on."

The big fish answer to the small fish. That's what Warren's mentor, Nathan Voloshen, had liked to say. The small fish were the ones who would protect you from the big fish. The small fish—the party officers, the county and state bureaucrats—were the ones who enabled the big fish—the judges, the politicians—to live out their public lives.

At Voloshen's level, it was the New York Stock Exchange, it was building highways in Florida, it was doing favors for the Duvalier government in Haiti. Voloshen was an attorney and lobbyist who did his deals not on K Street but right inside the office of the U.S. Speaker of the House, John McCormack. He had brought Warren to Washington, D.C., just a few days after Warren's parole in 1960, and had had him put his feet up on McCormack's desk. He had asked him how it felt. It had felt like a veil of immunity. Some alchemy of odors and fabrics and dark mahogany had made the law seem a perfect abstraction, a power you partook of by desecration, by putting your feet up on a congressman's desk and dialing a number on his phone.

A year later, he was in Phoenix. Five years later, he was a millionaire.

3

David Rich was speaking to his accountant, Ed Lazar, the door closed on an office covered in framed citations for contributions to Israel and local charities. Rich was a small, neat man with an animated face and cheerfully mischievous eyes. His dark suit, and the solemnity of what they were discussing, were somehow lightened by his East London accent, which sounded almost Australian.

"I watched Lee Ackerman turn into someone I didn't recognize," he said, leaning back in his chair. "I've known him for eighteen years. Most of that time we were in business together. He was handsome, he had a good head for numbers, you couldn't help but like Lee. But then he came to me before Diamond Valley's collapse and asked me to buy twenty-five thousand dollars of mortgages."

They were worthless—Ackerman had mortgaged the same piece of land two or three times, thinking, perhaps, that it didn't matter, that since the time payments were so small, no one was ever going to take title anyway. But half of the mortgages weren't even current. Rich had lost the whole $25,000.

Ed ran his hand over his knee, looking down, assessing the story because it didn't jibe with what he thought he knew. Dave Rich had been one of his clients for the past several years. It was only this week that he had learned of his connection to Ned Warren. He was trying to remember a series of newspaper stories from the year before—1967—about Warren and Ackerman, the kind of thing you skimmed if you read it at all, letting the photos and their captions do most of the work: "Lee J. Ackerman, Politician, Investor," "Nathan J. Warren, Two Prison Terms." It was the kind of story that left a strong but blunt impression, enough to muster an opinion about if it came up in conversation but not enough to support that opinion. He remembered there were some fraudulent deals. Selling land in a bar, phony sales. He remembered something about Warren's prison record. He'd been in Sing Sing. Ed remembered that.

"Ned was into all kinds of rackets," Rich said, breathing out in disgust. "But this was years ago, fifteen years ago. I understand, I did some checking up on him, too. He's in business with Richard Stenz now—Richard's some sort of higher-up in the Republican Party, very straight. Before I made any loans, I talked to Richard and he told me that Ned was completely reformed. Now, I agree with him, but I also understand your concerns. It wasn't Ned, though, it was Lee who came in here and sold me those twenty-five thousand dollars of bad mortgages."

"Where is Ackerman now?"

"Lee? It's a tragedy—the company's in bankruptcy, he's in personal bankruptcy. His house is on the market. The last I saw him, he wouldn't sit down, he was so anxious. Lee was never anxious."

Ed nodded slowly, his eyes moving away from Rich to the pictures on his wall. "Warren's books look fine," he said. "The last audit was Arthur Andersen. They're not exactly in the business of lying for people, not for people like Warren anyway."

"I told Ned you were my accountant," said Rich, clasping his hands on his desk and leaning forward. "I recommended you, and I wouldn't have done that if I thought Ned was a crook. He's made a pile of money in the last few years—Prescott Valley, this Queen Creek venture with Stenz. It's in his own interest to keep on the straight and narrow, don't you think?"

They're not exactly in the business of lying for people, not for people like Warren anyway.

It was a stupid thing to say, Ed thought in the car later that afternoon. The question it raised, of course, was why was Warren looking for a new accountant in the first place? Was it because Arthur Andersen had been too "conservative"?

He was on Camelback Road, driving to Warren's house in Paradise Valley. He had spoken to Warren that afternoon on the phone and told him yes, they had a deal, he would bring over some initial paperwork they could go over together. He had done this without thinking it through all the way, or rather he had wanted to do it and had allowed himself to make the call before working through all of his misgivings. It was a big account. If they took it on, it would be one of Gallant, Farrow's biggest accounts. Sam Gallant himself had encouraged Ed to give it his consideration.

When he'd hung up the phone, Ed had realized that he was curious about Warren in a way he would not have expected. He'd realized that he was looking forward to seeing Warren at his house instead of at his office.

He found the street he was looking for, North Dromedary Road, but then strayed off it, not in any hurry, wanting to just drive for a while, to look at the surroundings, the city's wealthiest neighborhood. The desert was still a vivid presence there, pink sand between the spacious two- or three-acre lots—vivid, but tamed. There were palm trees, paloverde trees, brilliant red bougainvillea draped over walls the color of mud. It was quiet, no other cars out. Trails led up to the boulder formations at the foot of Camelback Mountain, but no one was out walking on them. He finally got back on North Dromedary Road and began following its switch-backs up the mountainside, the road steeper and steeper, until he was almost unable to move any farther. Piles of crushed rock blocked the way in places, and slopes of crushed rock spilled off the edge, over the sheer, hundred-yard drop down the mountain-side. He saw a gated driveway and wondered if that was the turn-off he was looking for, East Grandview Lane, Warren's street. He put the parking brake on and got out of the car and took a closer look but could see nothing except extended driveway through the bronze grillwork.

He sat in the car for a moment, frustrated. If he went far-ther up, there was no guarantee he would be able to turn back around—his car was a large Pontiac sedan—and eventually he decided he might have missed the turn, and so he began the dif-ficult task of backing his way down, using the side mirror to keep the edge of the road in sight. It turned out that he had passed East Grandview Lane on his way up the mountainside. East Grand-view Lane was smoothly paved. He could see what he guessed was Warren's house beyond a curve in the road lined with perfectly spaced date palms. 4958 East Grandview Lane. He parked the car and took his briefcase and walked around the bougainvillea-covered wall to the low pale green rotunda where the front door was. Thin white columns held up the roof, whose greenness turned out to be the verdigris of weathered copper. He did not use words like *verdigris*. He did not look at the house, with its graceful, botany-inspired details, and think of Frank Lloyd Wright. It struck him as an unusually pleasant, understated house, a kind of ideal house he had never seen or thought of or imagined before.

"You must be Ed Lazar," a woman said, answering the doorbell. She was attractive, tanned, thin, her blond hair held loosely in a clip. Behind her, two black Dobermans were barking and pawing the carpeted floor. "Boys, stop it," she said, twisting toward them, a cigarette cocked at a perfect right angle to her hip. "Down." She looked at him again with a flat grin, a thin bar of flawless white teeth. "I'm Barbara Warren."

Inside, the front room was like an observation deck, its curved walls and floor-to-ceiling windows offering a protected sense of distance from the view outside, all of Phoenix stretched out beyond the palm-lined mountainside. There was the secretive hush of wealth—artwork, Navajo rugs, dark wooden furniture—everything kept clean and ordered by someone else, there for your enjoyment, there for you to use or just to look at. She showed him back into a den with a wall made of bare slate-colored rock—the actual side of Camelback Mountain—and then into a sunroom with opened windows, their iron frames painted brown. There were terra-cotta pots filled with geraniums, gardenias, jasmine. At the back of the room was a white bar shaped like a teardrop, where Barbara Warren poured him a Scotch, took his briefcase and jacket, and then showed him outside.

Warren was sitting at a glass table by the pool beneath an umbrella, reading a paperback novel and fingering a tall blue glass beaded with condensation. The table was covered with newspapers—the *Arizona Republic* and the *Phoenix Gazette*, the *Wall Street Journal* and the *New York Times*—an ashtray, cigarettes, a yellow pad and pen. He wore a clean white robe and espadrilles. His damp hair was slicked back after a swim in the pool. With his deep tan, the robe hanging open as he backed up his chair and stood to say hello, the impression he gave was of a man who had been everywhere and had laid out every aspect of his current life with a deliberate sense of what the options were.

"I heard you saw Dave Rich today," he said.

"I met with Dave this morning."

"He has a good accent. Everyone loves him for that accent."

"He was telling me about Lee Ackerman. Your old friend, or your old nemesis. I still don't understand the story."

Warren put his hand on Ed's shoulder and led him to the glass table. "Let's talk," he said. "I want to talk to you about this because I think you'll understand it from a business angle. You know the language—I don't think most people understand the language very well. Very few do anyway. It's boring, it doesn't make sense to them."

The weather was bright and warm, and the pale water in the pool shimmered—blurry, blue lattices forming and unfolding on the surface. Ed put his Scotch down on the table, rolled up his sleeves, sat down in the shade of the umbrella. Warren lit a cigarette. They talked for almost two hours. Barbara came out periodically to freshen their drinks and would sometimes lean for a while on Warren's chair and listen to what he was saying, silent, thoughtful. At one point, there was a clamor inside when the children came home from school. The Dobermans got out, racing around and then into the pool until Warren clapped his hands and they panted and bobbed around the glass table, shaking water from their gleaming backs. One of Warren's daughters came to take the dogs back inside, a pretty, blond girl who said hello and did a stiff pretend curtsy, laughing, the formal gesture some sort of joke between her and her father. When she went back inside, Warren reclined further in his chair.

"Lee Ackerman had no sense of timing," he said. "He bought

my shares at a bad time. It's not a beauty pageant, it's business, but everything I've done here is legal."

Ed looked out at the pool, then up and across the mountainside, the houses hanging like small fortresses out of the rock, the blue sky above them. He had finished a second and then a third Scotch. "I don't see how anyone stays in the land business for very long," he said. "I don't like the way the financing works. To me, it seems like it gets very close to a Ponzi scheme sometimes."

"Eighteen months," Warren said. "I like to build up a company for about eighteen months and then I like to sell it to someone else. After that, you really need someone who can manage money, someone who knows how to structure a company's finances. I like making money, but I'm not an accountant."

Ed smiled. "You're not an accountant. What's that supposed to mean?"

"You know what it means."

"No, I don't," Ed said, not smiling anymore.

"I guess it means that I don't know how you can stand doing taxes every year for some of the people you must have to work for. That's what it means. You don't seem like the type."

"It's not so bad."

"It's steady work. I understand that. Maybe I'm too much the other extreme. That's what used to get me into trouble."

It had all come out in their conversation—Warren's wayward past, the stories from a dozen years ago, twenty years ago, from when he was, for lack of a better term, a grifter. He had raised money for a concert for the blind, but the concert had never happened. He had found backers for a Broadway musical that also had never happened, though he had produced a script and a title—*The Happiest Days*—and billed Lucille Ball and June Allyson as the stars and hired a famous publicist, Chick Farmer, to promote it in the newspapers. He had spent a year in Sing Sing for *The Happiest Days*. You pictured him in a prison suit with a number on his chest, sawing his way through the bars with a file taken out of a cake—that was how real the time in Sing Sing seemed. It was hard to connect it to the fifty-three-year-old man sitting by the pool in his robe, a man who'd been to Europe, to New York, to Asia, a man whose financial statement linked him to some of the most important people in Phoenix—a man who understood the detailed complexities of his financial statement. To take his past seriously seemed to imply a lack of a sense of humor, a missing sense of joie de vivre. He was like Dean Martin, Ed thought. He had Dean Martin's thick crest of hair and his low-key, half-shrugging delivery. Like Dean Martin, he came across as a charming rogue, a man who had lived through all manner of disorder and yet had managed to land on his feet.

Barbara came out again, not to freshen their drinks this time but holding a tray with a great pitcher of ice water and some glasses. There were napkins so white they left a blind spot in your field of vision for a moment. There was a silver bowl of guacamole with peeled shrimp arrayed along the rim.

"We're having some guests come by for dinner in a little while," she said to Ed. "Around eight o'clock. Would you like to join us? I was thinking you could call your wife and see if she wanted to join us, too. I realize it's very short notice."

Ed sat with his hands on the aluminum arms of his deck chair. He had lost track of the time, but now he roused himself. "I'm sorry," he said. "I should let you get ready."

"Don't be ridiculous."

"No, of course. I really have to go anyway. We have a baby at home, I shouldn't have stayed so long."

Warren was reaching for a shrimp. Barbara was standing

behind him with her hand on his shoulder, as if to balance herself, while she inhaled from her cigarette.

Ed stood up and shook their hands. Then Barbara followed him into the sunroom, where he found his briefcase and his jacket and said a last good-bye. A part of him had wanted to stay for dinner, he realized. It surprised him that a part of him had wanted to stay for dinner.

4958 East Grandview Lane

4

Their neighborhood was tract houses. You picked one of five models from a book and then six months later you had neighbors who all had kids and bicycles and two cars.

"I can't believe we're living in a Norman Rockwell neighborhood," he said one day to Susie out of nowhere—one of those sudden views into something deeper that she had gotten accustomed to by now, Ed's occasional urge for something more or something else. She didn't know what to say, what more or what else could really make him any happier. They had a son, Zachary, whom he doted on, and his relationship with his other son, Richie, was different now, infused with his new understanding of what it meant to be a father. He played tennis several times a week, the game at his level an intense blending of the physical and the mental, a rapid blur of angles and approaches, satisfying, exhausting. On Saturday nights during football season, they went to the ASU games, the men in slacks and button-down shirts, the women in skirts and nylon stockings, all of that clothing in the 90-degree heat; and then afterward, during a late dinner and drinks in a Mexican restaurant, the darkness and coolness were soothing, you felt you were on vacation, that your life itself contained many of the elements of a vacation. It was a weekend life, an after-work life. It seemed perfect to him almost all of the time, as long as he was in it and not in his office.

It was not that he wanted material things: a boat, a second home, a luxury car. Things didn't interest him—what they signified had begun to interest him. In the office, there were subtle, newly unexpected humiliations that went along with the servicing of clients. They always wanted you to keep in mind, through a kind of code, how much money they made in relation to how much money you made. The code was simple—your car, the neighborhood you lived in, the stocks you owned, the pastimes you pursued. In the Midwest, no one would have questioned you about these subjects with such hungry interest. In Phoenix, because it was sunny, because you could play tennis every month of the year, could swim and play golf every month of the year, there was a competition to be more fun-loving, more free-spirited than everyone else. There are very few people in America who don't want to be fun-loving, free-spirited—Ed was both of these things by nature, he didn't have to pursue them. But he was learning, as people learn in all times and places, that the easiest way to remain fun-loving and free-spirited is to have a lot of money.

What he wanted was to not feel invisible, to not feel like he was failing just because he didn't want or have the boat, the second house, the better car.

Eighteen months, Warren had said—many times, in the months after their first meeting. In the land business, you can make $1 million in eighteen months. Ed and Susie went to a party at the Warrens' one Saturday, and the food, the table settings, the bossa nova music carried over the hidden patio speakers, had been of an elegance they'd never seen. There were people whose names you read in the newspaper—Richard Stenz, John Roeder—men in madras shirts and slacks and loafers. There was the ogre-like commissioner, J. Fred Talley, surrounded by men who did not look quite like businessmen, with their big lapels and turquoise watchbands and cologne. It was Phoenix. It was the city they lived in, the gaudy jumble of high and low, aspiration and bad taste, the very center of it, never before glimpsed from this close up. One of the land salesmen arrived in a Rolls-Royce. There was nothing in the world more ludicrous than a man in Arizona driving a Rolls-Royce—even Warren thought so—but the sense of how easy it would be to transform everything about your life, the sense of fun, that was something to think about.

It was the sense of fun that got him and Susie thinking.

July 20, 1969—the night of the moon landing. On the television, Neil Armstrong was walking on the cratered surface, his back hunched beneath his pack, arms out at the sides, skipping beside the planted American flag with great, hulking steps like a boy having fun. In Houston, the engineers watched him with concealed excitement, a control room full of almost identical men in white short-sleeved shirts and black neckties. They were the likable face of America—not napalm, not Agent Orange, but the boy's dream of space travel made real by the grown-up boy's practical science. "I just want to evaluate the different paces that a person can make traveling on the lunar surface," Armstrong said in his ordinary voice, bounding from side to side, watching his feet. "You do have to be rather careful to keep track of where your center of mass is. Sometimes it takes two or three paces to make sure you've got your feet underneath you." The flag and his giant steps made the moon seem toylike, their position on it central, a distant, eerie playground in a vast desert of white dust and crumbled rock. To stop himself from moving, Armstrong shifted out to the side a few steps and "cut a little," as he said, "like a football player."

At Ed and Susie Lazar's, on West San Miguel, they watched it several times, replay after replay. There was a deli tray on a long table—corned beef, pastrami, turkey, salami—a group of friends gathered in the living room before the television. Walter Cronkite was in the midst of a marathon thirty-hour broadcast. Walter Cronkite, as fatherly as God, was acting tonight like an awestruck boy. "Go, baby, go!" he'd yelled on lift-off. He was almost speechless when the *Apollo* first landed, touching down on the surface, as unreal as a dream but in fact real.

"I've grabbed the brass ring," Ed said when there was a lull in the action, when they had shown the sequence of Armstrong's walk yet again. "I got my real estate license. Ned and I are going into the land business."

There was silence. No one knew what to say at first. They had not been privy to the evolution of Ed's feelings toward Ned Warren, and for many of them the announcement came as a shock. They remembered his skepticism, then an amused interest, but not a real interest. Ed had always spoken about the land business in a denigrating or sarcastic tone—it's a bit of a racket, it comes close to a Ponzi scheme—and they had always shrugged and said, It's Arizona, it's the Wild West, anything goes. Everyone used that phrase, "It's the Wild West." Everyone used it and no one took it very seriously.

"That's terrific," someone said.

"Good for you, Ed."

He took a sip of his drink. "One small step for Ed Lazar."

He had been to a fortune-teller's booth a few days before, with Beverly Fineberg, the wife of his friend Ron. Beverly had asked a surprisingly solemn question. Her father had died when she was young, so she asked if she would live to see her grandchildren. The fortune-teller assured her that, yes, she would, there would be many years with her grandchildren. Perhaps to lighten the mood, Ed had asked a more facetious question: Would he be a millionaire by the time he was forty? The fortune-teller had heard this question many times before, always from men, and it was not a question she liked. She had a ready answer. "Yes," she said, "but the cost will be very high."

At all times, the most unlikely situations are unfolding all around us. It is our own luck that allows us not to see it. Our luck allows us not to see the people in the shadows, or not to see them as they really are. It is the people in the shadows who see us as we really are.

5

A kind of conjuration.

I am writing this sentence on June 21, 2007, almost exactly thirty-eight years after the night of the moon landing. I did not know the story of that night until a few months ago. Nine months ago, I knew almost nothing about my father at all. I am working from a stack of index cards, a time line filled out with notes taken in libraries and government agencies and in the room of my house that I use as a study. I have a banker's box full of newspaper clippings, depositions, grand jury testimony, office correspondence. I have the interviews I did with journalists and former police officers, with my parents' friends and relatives, with my mother. I have anecdotes like the one about the fortune-teller, the one about the night of the moon landing. I am trying to imagine how it all happened, trying to dramatize the scattered bits of information, to understand the nuances. I don't know if anyone who knew my father will recognize this portrait I'm making. This portrait is crucially distorted by the way his life ended. When his friends and loved ones knew him, they didn't know the future—the future had not yet distorted his image. I am adhering to the final shape, the unbeautiful shape of what happened, reconstructing an old mosaic with only a few of the tiles, letting the fragments suggest what might have been in the missing spaces.

Verde Lakes, Yavapai County, 2006

. . .

By the time I got to the exit to Camp Verde, it was snowing so hard that I could hardly discern the road from the empty land on either side of it. I didn't know quite where I was going. The wipers were moving at full speed. There was a road called General Crook's Trail, and I followed this road into an Old West town where the buildings, as much as I could see of them, were outsize brick or wood facades in front of rough, windowless boxes. There was a café, a title company, a store. I drove up and down the main street and finally pulled into the parking lot of the title company. It was snowing even harder by then, the sky getting darker, the day seeming to end already though it was not yet noon. A secretary told me there might be someone at the chamber of commerce who could give me a better map of the area. She knew where Verde Lakes was, but her directions were confusing. The chamber of commerce was staffed by an elderly woman with an odd, comical way of speaking that turned out to be unintentional. She wore a vest and owlish glasses and moved around in a determined way, finally providing me with a flier that had a vague map with stars on it for the area's restaurants and motels. It wasn't surprising to hear her story of dropping everything to come to this part of Arizona. She told me that she knew some people who lived in Verde Lakes. She said it was a shame what had happened there. The land, she said, had been sold as a retirement village to air force pilots stationed in Japan. Some of the lots were in a flood zone. She told me there'd been a terrible flood several years ago, in the 1980s, in which a woman died, pets were abandoned, garbage was left strewn in the limbs of trees. "I remember when that was still a ranch and I went up to Ned Warren and I asked him what he was doing building on a flood plain," she said. "He told me the water never gets that high."

She didn't know my father's name. I had talked to enough people in Arizona by then to not be surprised that she remembered Ned Warren. I left the chamber of commerce with the map and went back to my car. By then, there was a good three inches of snow and I was getting concerned about whether I'd be able to drive back to Phoenix if the storm persisted. I didn't want to spend the night in Camp Verde. I drove with the radio off so I could concentrate better on the road. Verde Lakes was about a seven-minute drive from the chamber of commerce. Down the highway a few more miles was a state park and a little farther down was an Indian reservation casino, but Verde Lakes itself was just some land near nothing, a few trees and a grid of streets that looked like it had sat vacant for a long time before gradually accommodating a few trailers and simple one-story houses. It went on and on, block by block, a suburban neighborhood that had failed to appear—no homes in different styles, no landscaping or patios or decks. A school bus dropped off a few kids. Later, some teenagers walked by in black clothes and camouflage, part of a six-pack on a plastic tree, cigarettes. I was taking pictures of their neighborhood and I don't know what that meant to them, or if it meant anything at all. They looked at me in my car and they became alert, self-conscious, their suspicion visibly turning from me to themselves.

There was a street there, as I knew there would be, called Zachary Lane. My mother had always told me about Zachary Lane, about how my father, in the early days of his land company, had named a street after me. There was another, longer street called Lazar Road: vacant lots, trailers, fences made of wire and stakes. On one of the street signs someone had taped up a home-made poster for a yard sale.

I've grabbed the brass ring.

I didn't know the story of the brass ring or the moon landing on that day, but I sensed that this was not the kind of place my father had imagined. But perhaps he had simply not cared—perhaps I was naive about his motives or intentions. I knew I was not an objective judge. My emotions were carrying me from one conjecture to another. His life and death seemed pointless in that place. I thought he must have been either very foolish or very cynical, but neither view was very convincing.

Months later, I came across a memo from a journalist about my father.

Several different profiles have emerged of Lazar—a "sheep," an aggressor, a devoted husband, a swinger—but no one seems sure which description fits the best.

PART TWO

A Phoenix attorney who dealt with Warren during his early land dealings says a favorite Warren saying was: "Everybody's crooked—I'll show you." Said the lawyer: "Corrupting people—this was his delight."

—Newsday, March 23, 1977

6

Mexico—somewhere on the Pacific coast, perhaps Mazatlán, not that long a flight from Phoenix. The date is easier to determine: it would have been Saturday, August 14, 1971. At a beach resort somewhere in Mexico, Ned Warren was sitting on the patio with a woman named Acquanetta Ross, waiting for his wife, Barbara, and Acquanetta's husband, Jack, to come back from the concierge desk. Acquanetta Ross was dressed in a red cape, with peacock feathers in her hair, a beauty mark painted on her cheek. Like her name, her appearance was gaudy, theatrical, but her dark hair and sharp cheekbones projected a seriousness, even a toughness. She used a silver spoon to push a slice of lemon into a cup of plain hot water. She was dieting; this was part of her diet, she kept saying.

"What did Jack say about the land?" she asked.

"He said he bought some land yesterday. He said there was a balloon payment coming up down the road and he was already worried about it."

"That's all he's talked about. I asked him why did he buy the land if he was going to worry about this balloon payment. It's really ridiculous, don't you think, these words they come up with? Balloon payment."

"I'd say it's a pretty descriptive word," Warren said.

She stared at him with a showy disdain, blowing out smoke from her cigarette. "I can't read my watch," she said. "Where are they? What time is it?"

"It's a little after seven."

"I can't stand wearing glasses. I know it's vain, but I won't wear them."

She had been a B actress in Hollywood once, a star in films with titles like *Captive Wild Woman*, or *Tarzan and the Leopard Woman*. These feral roles had fallen to her because of her dark skin. For a time, her handlers had called her "The Venezuelan Volcano," though in fact she was not Venezuelan but Arapaho Indian. Warren knew the story, as did most of what passed for "society" in Phoenix. The Indian blood was the subject of disdain, even if she and her husband, Jack, were local celebrities of a kind. Jack Ross's Lincoln/Mercury dealership sponsored a weekly horror movie that Acquanetta presented on TV, dressed in outlandish costumes. On the strength of those ads, Jack was mounting a campaign for governor—laugh, but it was Arizona. Jack Ross's brother, as Warren well knew, was married to the daughter of the most powerful man in Arizona, Barry Goldwater. There were reasons for this conversation.

"I wouldn't worry about the balloon payment," he said. "I have some investors over in Japan, they're desperate for land."

"Japan. Why would anyone in Japan want to buy land in Yavapai County?"

"They're Americans. It's a company that sells land to American G.I.s. Do you know how many soldiers are stationed in Japan? Korea, the Philippines?"

"No."

"I never would have thought of it myself. Soldiers. Every one of those soldiers needs a place to invest his money."

In six months, Acquanetta Ross would deny this conversation ever happened. In six months, Jack Ross would deny the entire trip to Mexico had ever happened. Eventually, these denials would create a mystery as to how Ed Lazar had known to call Jack Ross sometime in early September 1971 about some land Ross owned in Yavapai County, land that Ed Lazar had never seen, land that perhaps no one but Jack Ross ever really saw.

My father and Warren had offices on Camelback Road, in a bland stretch of small, nondescript buildings housing garages and stores. I have what I think must be a false memory of going there as a child: a door with the words *Consolidated Mortgage Corporation* printed film noir–style on its opaque glass panel, my father moving boxes of file folders through the door into the trunk of his car. I've had this memory for many years—I don't know what it means. It comes back periodically, without connection to anything in my current life, and though it seems suggestive, it also seems meaningless, interesting but only spuriously so.

I have some of my father and Warren's business correspondence to each other, which sounds like this:

> On Cornwall forget unit 2 temporarily—suggest we
> keep those lots—I get his inventory—
>   on mobile lots—suggest Cornwall keep the down
> to 10% —we require 10% down—

leaves balance average of $3600—we want $1000
plus the interest so we take
    correct percentage of flow starting 1st month—
On Com'l same thing according to a formula on the
individual lot or if you prefer on the average lot with a
    restriction that in no event should the impound
on the individual lot be less than $1000 (plus int.)

A strange and difficult poem, written in unfamiliar language. I have read it many times now, and read many pages like it in order to understand some of its meaning, through context and association. Like a poem, it became more interesting over time, every word significant, every phrase set down with authority.

They were not fools, nor were they unsophisticated. They were slowly building up a business on margin, figuring out ways to eke out a profit, calculating the percentages. After two years of patient work, it seemed as if it was finally going to pay off, and perhaps that was why they decided to reward themselves that fall of 1971. What ends up being called "greed" seldom looks like greed at the time; it looks like common sense, ambition.

Warren liked Ed Lazar—he liked his surprising spark, his sense of strategy. He liked the feeling you got that in some private way Ed's life was geared toward obtaining and savoring a good time. He could look up and say one deadpan phrase that made you laugh, or he could say nothing, his eyes still, his silence the only sign of his disagreement. Without Ed Lazar's image, it would have been impossible to underwrite Consolidated Mortgage Corporation with loans from places like First National Bank or ITT or Westinghouse. Without his acumen, it would have been impossible to turn a profit without resorting to financial corner-cutting or outright fraud.

They were playing it basically straight, taking out loans instead of selling mortgages, using the loans to put in the improvements on the land—the roads, the water lines, the utilities. The business was not a Ponzi scheme but an actual land development company. It was a slow grind: taking out loans brought in less cash than selling mortgage paper. But that May—May of 1971—Warren had walked into David Rich's office and announced that he and Ed Lazar were both about to make $1 million.

Rich turned a memo at a right angle to mark its place in a stack of papers. "You found a buyer," he said.

"In California. Out in Bakersfield. They're called American Home Industries. AHI. They build modular homes—it's a good match for them, they can sell the land and then sell the homes."

"That's terrific, Ned. You've done really well, you and Ed."

"They might be interested in that land of yours out near Casa Grande. I'll speak to them if you want."

"Acting as their broker, I suppose."

Rich smiled and had the secretary bring in a bottle of Johnnie Walker and two glasses. This was how Consolidated Mortgage had started, with a glass of Scotch in the office of David Rich, who had loaned them the money—$30,000 that was now somehow worth more than $2.5 million in American Home Industries stock. Thirty thousand dollars that Rich had loaned them at a usurious 18 percent interest, the maximum allowed by law.

"You and Ed must be over the moon," Rich said.

"Over the moon."

"Happy, fulfilled. Not your style, I know. You want me to go in on the deal too, is that it?"

Warren raised a hand slightly above his knee. "Your choice. I just wanted you to know about it. After that eighteen percent loan, I thought maybe you thought we didn't know what we were doing, Ed and I."

. . .

It was only on paper, but there were things about being a paper millionaire that made your life easier right away. The risk was over, for one thing: the risk of lot buyers defaulting, the risk of Warren losing patience and sending the salesmen out to manufacture bad contracts. They had done a stock swap with American Home Industries, and now AHI was going to pay them a bimonthly salary in addition to giving them $2.5 million worth of its shares. Suddenly money seemed easy to make, a trick you had already pulled off once. Like winning at cards, it made you feel you had some special skill, a feeling that was hard to resist, even when you saw its illogic. That winter, Arizona State had won the Peach Bowl after an undefeated season, and it sometimes seemed like a good omen, a prophecy of what came about that spring.

The author's father (in the rear in white shirt) and mother (beside him), after the Peach Bowl

Ed didn't touch the money. The neighbors had all installed fences for privacy, but Ed didn't bother—his entire property remained exposed. He didn't understand the need for those fences. What could anyone be doing that required so much privacy? That was how he lived as a millionaire—shooting baskets at the local high school, riding there on his bike—not telling anyone about the success, instead savoring his own tact.

> The name of Senator Barry Goldwater, Republican of Arizona, has twice cropped up in the current investigation....
>
> The Arizona Republic published copies of letters written in 1971 by Mr. Goldwater and [U.S. Congressman Sam] Steiger on their official stationery endorsing one of Mr. Warren's projects called Chino Valley Ranchettes, that was offered to American servicemen abroad under terms that violated Arizona law. The Phoenix Police Department said they had evidence that the actual wording of the letter had been drafted by Mr. Lazar.
>
> The letters were used in sales promotion of the land, which the Phoenix police later found to be without water and with rock conditions that made installation of functioning septic tanks impossible.
>
> —*New York Times*, June 14, 1976

They had demonstrated an ability to turn over land, to buy it cheaply and sell it quickly, and now there was a whole new market opening up, a company called Capital Management Systems

based in Koza, Okinawa, that sold to servicemen all across the
Far East—Japan, Taiwan, the Philippines, Guam. They didn't
spend much time marveling at the exotic sound of Koza, Okinawa. What mattered to Ed and Warren was that Capital Management Systems had bought lots in Verde Lakes and now they
were going to buy many more lots in Consolidated's new subdivision, Chino Meadows, in an area called Chino Valley, in central Yavapai County, near Prescott. The names would turn out
to be confusing: Chino Meadows, Chino Valley. Many people
would mix up the different "Chinos." It made it still more confusing that Capital Management Systems was in Japan. But
what mattered was the size of the market. *Soldiers. Every one of
those soldiers needs a place to invest his money.* Consolidated,
their firm, would go from being a retailer to a wholesaler, dealing in large volumes with Capital Management Systems, not the
former lot-by-lot drudgery with all its attendant risks. What was
even better was that they could make these deals on the side, out
of the purview of their buyer, AHI, because Warren had somehow
persuaded AHI to remove the noncompete clause from the
contract. This meant they had AHI credit lines, but they also
had the ability to go in on separate deals, to set up separate
corporations.

Capital Management Systems was called CMS. Consolidated
Mortgage Corporation was called CMC. The new umbrella
they began to work under was called Consolidated Acceptance
Corporation, or CAC, a separate corporation from CMC. It was
going to be very hard for people to keep track of what was what
or who was who: CAC, CMC, CMS. As it went forward, even
the secretaries would sometimes get the different letterheads
mixed up.

．　．　．

Warren stacked some papers on his desk, his forehead still shiny from the heat outside. He had just returned from his long weekend on the beach in Mexico. He wore a tan suit and a pale blue shirt and he sucked on a Dum Dum lollipop because he was trying to cut down on his smoking.

"I get bored on the beach after about ten minutes," he said. "Nothing to do." He was in his Robert Mitchum mode, dapper and sarcastic, breezing into the office now to check his mail, then breezing to his other offices, then back to his house and the pool.

Ed sat down in one of his chairs. He could play this game as long as Warren wanted to. He wasn't going to be the one who mentioned the letter that had just arrived that morning from Barry Goldwater.

"How was the marijuana down there?" he said.

Warren pretended to shiver. "No comment."

"Well, at least you got out of this inferno for a few days."

"I may have a lead on some more land. Straight brokerage deal. No financing, no salesmen, nothing."

"Where?"

"Near Chino. It would be a good favor for us to do. But let's worry about Chino first." He examined his lollipop, glaring at it for not being a cigarette. "This one's called Chino, too, actually. Chino Something-Else. Chino Grande."

Ed knew Warren was waiting for him to bring up the Goldwater letter. He knew Warren knew he was thinking this. It was a game they played, a telepathy of withholding, in some ways more important than whatever words they ever actually spoke. When they spoke, it was jokes, banter, cocktail talk, punctuated by a two-minute phone call or a terse memo written almost anonymously. *Got it*, was the only note Warren had appended to the Goldwater letter, for, as they both appreciated, any further comment would only diminish the impact of the signature at the bottom: just the first name, *Barry*, in firm blue ink.

Ed had been in the men's room that morning when Fred Greene, the collections agent, had come in and walked over to the urinal. Greene was six six and weighed almost three hundred pounds, standing there with both hands on his hips, the man who knocked on doors when a mortgage went unpaid.

"Your salesmen are all worried about their jobs," he said, scowling down as if pissing were a kind of indigestion. "They're all trying to make a hundred thousand in sales before their business gets shipped overseas to Japan or Taiwan or wherever the hell it is."

Ed stared into the mirror as he washed his hands. "They'll still have jobs," he said.

Greene flushed the urinal. His shoes were as big as galoshes, white with silver chains. "These guys would sell to a dead man if they could keep their commissions."

"Yeah, well, that's why we have Mean Fred Greene."

Greene moved toward the sink, pumped soap powder all over the basin, then washed his hands under full pressure from the tap. After pounding his hands dry on a thick stack of paper towels, he threw the towels on the floor by the wastebasket. Not in the basket, but on the floor.

Ed nodded, his silence a coded laugh that Greene acknowledged with more silence, not looking but seeing.

Ed thought, if the CMS deal worked and the lot sales happened in Japan instead of here, then he wouldn't have to think about any of this anymore—not the salesmen, not the commissions, not the stupidity, not the greed. He wouldn't have to see

Fred Greene tossing his garbage on the men's room floor. He would see numbers, contracts, memos, statements. He would take his seat on the board of AHI and after a reasonable amount of time had elapsed, he would sell his shares and get out of the business.

> Mr. Dave Martin
> Capital Management Systems Ltd., Inc.
> P.O. Box 364
> Koza, Okinawa
>
> Dear Dave:
>
> Best wishes on your investment program for the ownership of home-sites in Chino Valley, Arizona.
>
> Much of Arizona's phenomenal growth has been due to the fact that many service men that were based in Arizona during their training decided to make their home here in their civilian life. These men have contributed a great deal to the vitality and growth of our State. This program should be an additional step along these lines. We wish you continued success.
>
> With best wishes,
Barry Goldwater

Ed put it back in its manila envelope and looked again at the memo he'd written yesterday:

TO: N. J. Warren
FROM: Edward Lazar

We will want a letter from Sam Steiger that will read something like the following:

Mr. Dale Holmgren
Mr. Dave Martin
Mr. Dale Hunt
Mr. Harry Gillis

Capital Management Systems Ltd., Inc.
P.O. Box 364
Koza, Okinawa

Dear Mr. So and So:

Best wishes on your investment program for the owner-ship of home-sites in Chino Valley, Arizona.

Much of Arizona's phenomenal growth has been due to the fact that many service men that were based in Arizona during their training decided to make their home here in their civilian life. These men have contributed a great deal to the vitality and growth of our state. Your program should be an additional step along these lines. Continued success.

Sincerely,

Sam Steiger

"No one's heard of Sam Steiger," Warren had said on the phone yesterday, speaking from his house. "Sam Steiger's just a congress-man from Arizona."

"He's helping us out with the Forest Service," Ed had said.

"So get him, too," Warren had answered, as if with a shrug.

The memo had been delivered to Warren's house by messen-ger boy and then the letter had been dictated to Goldwater's office by someone over the phone—that was the only way it could have happened in less than twenty-four hours. That also explained some minor differences in a few of the sentences. But he couldn't imagine Warren patiently reading a letter over the phone, making subtle changes of phrasing. The phrases would have been changed by someone's secretary, probably Goldwater's, but how the letter had even made it that far was a mystery.

It was the Wild West—that was the phrase that covered such mysteries. He could have asked Warren how the Goldwater letter had materialized, how it had happened in less than twenty-four hours, but it was the kind of question you knew not to ask after two years in the land business. They had connections to a lot of people. Now they somehow had connections to Barry Goldwater. He wondered if not just Sam Steiger but Barry Goldwater owned land in Chino Valley.

———

"I need a favor," Jack Ross had said that afternoon in Mexico, standing at the bar, drinking whiskey because that was what he drank, even by a pool. "That land I told you about, I don't know what I'm going to be able to do with it."

Warren nodded. "It's called Chino Grande?"

"That's right. They did up a flier already. Chino Grande Ranchettes."

"Outside Seligman."

"Far outside. There's no road."

"But it's in Chino Valley."

"Not really Chino Valley. It's north of there."

"We'll call it Chino Valley. That way we'll keep it simple."

Their conversation would have happened on August 14. The Goldwater letter was dated August 19. The first time Warren mentioned the Jack Ross land to Ed Lazar was a month later, in September. There were reasons for doing it this way, reasons for spacing out the favors so that no one could connect them too easily.

CAC, CMC, CMS. Chino Valley, Chino Meadows, Chino Grande. This is how you can become a party to fraud without quite knowing it, without the perpetrator necessarily even planning it that way.

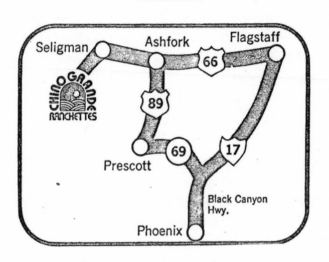

Ed drove home that evening in his new car. He liked it even less than his last car, which had been a Cadillac. Like the Cadillac, the new car, a Lincoln, had been Warren's idea. It made Ed feel silly—it was ostentatious, it cost more than his house was worth—but there was only so much you could explain to your friends and family about the performative aspects of the land business. At the Lincoln/Mercury dealership in Mesa, Jack Ross had gone over all the details before handing Ed the keys—the Kashmir Walnut Matina paneling, the Cartier timepiece, the small, oval-shaped "opera" windows in the back—all the details that made the Lincoln Continental Mark IV different from last year's Lincoln Continental Mark III. It had a grille in front, designed to mimic a Rolls-Royce's, and a rounded, old-timey hump in the rear where the spare tire fit. Ed pulled it into his driveway now and opened the garage door and hid it inside—he never left his company cars in the driveway. He turned his back on the closed garage and faced the sunlight.

It was 103 degrees, the heat a white sheen on the houses and the asphalt cul-de-sac. His son Zachary and Zachary's friend David Nichols were playing on a plastic slide hooked up to a garden hose in the front yard of David's house. He left his briefcase in the driveway and started walking toward them, knowing that he would get his suit pants wet when Zachary came running over. Susie and Carol must have been inside Carol's house in the air-conditioning. He would say hello and then he would go back home and change into his bathing trunks and he and the boys would splash around in the plastic pool in the backyard. That was what he wanted to do. It seemed remarkable, after getting out of that car on the day the Goldwater letter arrived, that this was what he wanted to do.

Acquanetta

7

October 3, 1971—about a month after Warren had flown to Tachikawa, Japan, to present the board members of CMS with photographs, a fact sheet, and a preliminary grid of Jack Ross's acreage of "green, rolling hills" at Chino Grande, outside Seligman. He had also brought a promotional letter from Senator Barry Goldwater, in gratitude for which CMS had offered Warren the loan of their spokesman, the actor Cesar Romero, who stood now under a white pavilion set up outside the clubhouse at Verde Lakes, greeting a kind of reception line of thirty or forty prospective buyers who had just arrived in a fleet of vans from Phoenix.

On their way to meet the former movie star and current supporting player on TV's *Alias Smith and Jones*, the prospective buyers could help themselves to a paper cup of fruit punch laid out on the buffet table covered in a plastic cloth held in place by clothespins. Cesar Romero shook their hands, bowing slightly forward at the waist, courtly, Latin. Many of the people in line remembered him from his days as a romantic lead, dancing with Carmen Miranda or Betty Grable. They remembered him as Hernan Cortez with a silver breastplate and flowing sleeves in *Captain from*

Castile. They were flattered to meet him, and his presence, along with the pennants and picnic tables and chairs, made the empty streets of Verde Lakes, some of them nothing more than dirt ruts, some still not even bladed by the bulldozer, look like the early growth of what would someday be a functioning town.

"He's worth the thousand dollars," said Harry Gillis of CMS, who had flown over from Japan that week to see Verde Lakes and Chino Meadows and Jack Ross's Chino Grande, which he would do tomorrow from Ross's private plane. Gillis was a handsome balding man with sideburns and an easy California smile. He had an enthusiasm for sports cars. He was bright, genial, but when Ed asked him a few token questions about his family, there emerged a murky picture of a wife and son back in Seattle whom he never saw. Money did odd things to people, made them migrate to Japan, but perhaps Gillis's move hadn't been for the money but for the distance. Gillis was an Irish name, Ed thought—Catholic, no possibility of divorce.

Cesar Romero made a blank face and bent down low to hear what an older woman was trying to communicate to him, her hand on his biceps, raising her chin, a white sun visor coming down over her forehead and large black-lensed sunglasses covering her eyes. She was a kind of woman Ed recognized: opinionated, not just unwilling but incapable of hearing anything that did not fit into her line of argument. She didn't realize that Romero knew even less than she did about Verde Lakes or Chino Meadows or the investment potential of real estate in Yavapai County.

"A thousand dollars a day," Ed said. "I guess basically he gets paid to feel ridiculous for a couple of hours."

"Acting. Just a different kind of acting," said Gillis.

"We can go inside the clubhouse and have a real drink if you want."

"No, I'm all right. I haven't seen one of these sales promos in a long time. I'm getting kind of a kick out of it."

Ed looked over toward a couple standing in line. "It's always geared toward the wife," he said. "The pitch, I mean. It's usually the wife who makes all the decisions. Either that, or she can't stand it when her husband looks like a cheapskate. The salesman hands her a notepad and he says, 'Write this down. You'll want to remember these figures.' It gets her used to following instructions. On the other hand, it makes her feel like she's important, the one in charge. The longer the husband says nothing, the more she starts to get interested in the whole project. You'd be surprised how much emotion these guys create. Anxiety. Humiliation. Then they say, 'Isn't it beautiful out here? Don't you just love the fresh air?' I've actually seen them sometimes—they'll bend down and pick up a handful of dirt and talk about how beautiful it is, how there's nothing like good, clean desert soil. The husband is standing there with this look on his face like his feet hurt. By then, the salesman looks like Tony Bennett compared to him. That's the way these deals work a lot of the time."

Gillis sniffed a little laugh and looked down at his shoes. "We do it mostly with brochures," he said, "brochures and promises." He looked around with something like a poetic squint. "Does it get very hot here in the summer?"

"It gets pretty hot. Not like Phoenix, but hot. In the hundreds."

"And what about Chino?"

"Chino's the same."

"There's trees, a water table. It's not like it's the sandy wastes."

"We'll take a drive over there after lunch. It looks like this. Trees, hills, more lush than maybe you'd expect."

"You're talking about Chino Meadow."

"Chino Meadows. With an *s*. I've never seen the other one, Chino Grande, but you'll see that tomorrow with Ross."

At a pair of large charcoal grills, a few cooks were flipping hamburgers onto plastic trays. The air smelled like burnt meat, lighter fluid, smoke. Pennants flapped in the breeze—white and green and yellow. There was a long table set up with ketchup, pickle relish, yellow mustard, bags of buns, and, still in their plastic crate, large bottles of Mr Pibb. Cesar Romero, as if dreading the imminence of this lunch, came over to say good-bye. He appeared unrealistically clean and pressed, his collar still bright white, his suit jacket buttoned. With his white hair and mustache, he looked not like the Joker he played on *Batman* but like an anchorman or a game show host. It was surprising, nevertheless, how strongly his fame asserted itself. He wore it like a glass panel through which everyone on the other side appeared amusing, harmless, neutral.

"I must go," he said. "Many thanks. It was a pleasure to meet you both."

"Thank you, Cesar," said Gillis.

"Thank you," said Ed.

Romero shook their hands. "This is very interesting. This development will be for trailers?"

"Some mobile homes, some houses," said Ed.

"Well, I wish you nothing but the best," Romero said, backing away. "We say in Spanish, *¡Te la comiste, hoy!*" He looked at the sky, breathing in through his nose. "It means, 'You ate it!'" He smiled. "But really it means, 'You've had a great success.' Really, a great success today. *¡Un triunfo grande!*"

He walked away, and Ed and Gillis didn't say anything.

"He actually thinks we're stupid," Gillis finally commented.

"I guess it would be hard to blame him."

"He bats for the other side, you know. That's basically an open secret."

Ed's secretary, Sharon, brought them over some plates of food once the prospective buyers had finished helping themselves. There was very little you would want to eat. Sharon herself had found some cottage cheese, but she would never have considered offering that to a man, so Ed and Gillis did their best with the gray hamburgers and the sweet beans in their puddles of sauce.

"Maybe I'll take you up on that drink after all," said Gillis.

They headed over toward the clubhouse. The sales team was offering door prizes to a dozen of the prospective buyers. The prizes were S & H Green Stamps, sheets of little stamps you pasted into a book and redeemed for merchandise. The winners of the stamps were also given blue ribbons—the salesmen pinned the ribbons onto their shirts, as if bestowing an honor, smiling at their own guile. The winners had been selected not at random but after the salesmen had had a chance to observe what they were like. The blue ribbons indicated easy marks—"mooks," in the parlance, "Mickey Nothings," "Johnny Zeroes." These were the ones you tried to sell not one but four or five lots, working out a financing plan, tying their heads in knots with complicated discounts and plans for resale with an eighteen-month option.

"I think you can see why we're interested in getting out of the retail side," Ed said.

Gillis nodded as he followed Ed into the shade of the clubhouse. He was chewing his burger and looking at his fact sheet for Chino Grande, holding it awkwardly beneath his paper plate. "You think we're better off just driving to Grande today after we see Meadow?" he said. "That way I could skip the plane ride tomorrow with Ross, maybe catch an earlier flight back to L.A."

Ed shrugged. "Honestly, I wouldn't know how to get there. I think they're still working on the road."

It came to him as they stepped into the clubhouse: the emptiness of Gillis. The sales meetings, the dinners in hotel rooms, the auditoriums, the airports. It was always better not to think too much about the lives of other men, especially those you didn't know very well, but he couldn't stop thinking about Gillis with a Scotch in a plastic cup, flying to California from Japan, then on to Phoenix—his toilet kit, his Robert Ludlum novel—all so that he could report back on this sales program in the desert. *Six thousand acres at two hundred per brings you to a million two plus commissions and fees.* He realized then that Gillis was not crooked but perhaps so bored and apathetic that he was in his own way a kind of risk.

Cesar Romero, with the author's grandparents, Louis and Belle Lazar

8

Not long after the AHI merger, Ed had come back to the office one afternoon to find one of his former sales managers, James Cornwall, waiting for him in his office. Cornwall's Rolls-Royce had been sitting in the parking lot, a white Silver Shadow with UK plates, a car he'd bought from Warren not long before this. Cornwall stood up when Ed came in, holding a hand to his stomach to keep his tie in place as he rose from his seat. There was something studied about the gesture, along with the expensive silk tie that picked up a deep navy thread in Cornwall's sport coat. He was tall, with a blond crest of hair slicked back with brillantine. It occurred to Ed that the more compromised a person became, the more compelled he was to draw attention to himself. Or perhaps it was the opposite: the showiness made you a "character," so colorful that no one, not even the authorities, took you very seriously. Cornwall was a deputy in something called the Sheriff's Posse, a fundraising group whose members were entitled to wear silver stars and ten-gallon hats like the lawmen to whom they wrote their checks.

"We missed you at the party last weekend," Cornwall said in friendly accusation.

Ed nodded, shaking his hand. "How was it?"

"Forty, fifty people. Janet King in a very interesting top."

They sat down, both of them unhappy, both of them trying to conceal it. A year ago, Cornwall had been the head of one of the least successful sales offices at Consolidated Mortgage. Now he had a house in Paradise Valley not far from Warren's, a house with a swimming pool and a tennis court, a view of Camelback Mountain. He had been installed by Warren as president of something called the Great Southwest Land and Cattle Company, a business that since its inception a year ago Ed had been doing his best to stay out of. Great Southwest had been the genesis of Warren's Consolidated Acceptance Corporation, a way he could bill Great Southwest for all the help it was getting with its operations—its billing, its articles of incorporation, its HUD applications. But the advice and help had never seemed to stop.

Cornwall had heard about the AHI merger.

"It sounds like you and Mr. Warren are going your separate ways," he said, crossing his legs.

"Not really. It's just a merger. We'll still be in charge of our own offices."

"But you won't be working for him anymore."

"He won't have the same control he had, if that's what you mean."

Cornwall cocked his head to one side. "I told Ned that's the kind of deal that would really help me, and he just smiled."

"Yeah. The smile."

"I could use the financing more than you could—you know that. If there's any way you could put in a word for me, I would appreciate it."

"We both know how much good that would do." He looked at Cornwall. "I told Ned that you and Great Southwest should be searching for ways to refinance, but he's not listening. We both know how that is. I think the real problems are going to come down the road, in six or seven months, so right now the best thing you could do is probably start pulling out."

"I was thinking something like that."

"I don't know how much you're on the hook for personally."

"I've got a lot of loans out there. A lot of notes with my signature on them."

Ed just stared at him. Cornwall smiled ruefully down at his knee. He seemed to be ruminating on his own foolishness but without taking it very seriously. The chain of mistakes was regrettable, but how could he have known, he was just an ordinary person, Mr. Warren had been making the real decisions. That was what he seemed to be telling himself, as if this would somehow mitigate the consequences. Never mind the house in Paradise Valley, the Rolls-Royce, the tennis court and pool. Never mind the huge salary package Warren had offered him right from the start, a man with little business experience and little ability with numbers. It was just dumb luck, the ill fate of someone giving things a go, seizing the main chance.

Ed turned away, his tongue pressing at the corner of his mouth. "Listen, I was glad to help you out with the HUD reports and the billing and the forms, but I have no say about what Warren wants you to do over there at this point. You know that."

"I understand."

"You can't bring me into it."

"There's just this hole opening up, bigger and bigger."

"It's going to get bigger still. Unfortunately, I think that might have been the plan."

When Cornwall left, Ed went down the hall to the men's room. He washed his hands and face and then he brushed and flossed his teeth. He dried off with a sheaf of paper towels, closing his eyes.

He had gone to the Peach Bowl in Atlanta that winter with Susie, Ted and Elaine Kort, the Minkoffs, the Segals. A few days before they'd left, Warren had come to him with a new business proposition, a way to bill for their expertise without risking any of their capital: a consulting business for other land companies, Consolidated Acceptance Corporation. Their first client could be James Cornwall, who was already struggling with the new venture Warren had set up for him, the Great Southwest Land and Cattle Company.

What was Warren like, people would ask, and Ed would say that he was a "character," he was "colorful," but also "brilliant," "charming," a kind of genius when it came to making deals. He always had dozens of them in progress—deals on land developments, commercial real estate, insurance—deals involving half a dozen prominent country club members and their attorneys, but also smaller, grittier deals—deals on soft drink distributorships, vending machines, taverns, liquor licenses, which as an ex-convict he was legally unable to hold. Ed would try to explain the layers of a personality like this, but there weren't many people who understood the nuances. There was the Warren who had everyone to his house parties—the buffet by the pool, the bartender in his white jacket—the Warren of the bright, cajoling smile, a half circle of guests surrounding him in front of the camera. There was the opposite Warren: the chain-smoker in his tattered golf shirt who scrutinized numbers, bank letters, accounting ledgers, who saw everyone, not least himself, as a little contemptible, a little disgusting in their simple motive of gain. There was the Warren of hangovers and there was the Warren of nights on the town at Rocky's Hideaway, Durant's, the Roman Gate Cocktail Lounge—girls in friends' apartments, girls in the Embassy Hotel.

There was the Warren who stopped by Ed and Susie's house like a bland uncle with a box of macadamia nuts from Hawaii, a case of Baileys Irish Cream, standing in the kitchen, asking Susie about the kids, remembering their names, remembering the toys they played with. He and Barbara would come over for dinner with Ed's parents and they would talk about the new biography of the Roosevelts, *Eleanor and Franklin,* about college football, about *Diamonds Are Forever,* the most ordinary family talk, the Warrens like film stars in the small dining room, distinguishing themselves by their total lack of aloofness. After dinner, while the women did the dishes, the men would drink Scotch in the living room, and then the women would join them for dessert. Even recounting the plot of a movie, Warren would keep everyone so engaged that Ed's parents, Lou and Belle, would stay late, Warren's energy becoming theirs, drawing them out, causing them to tell stories of their own, jokes of their own—Warren always laughed at their jokes. It was a strange mix of performance and actual kindness, the performance and the kindness rising to greater heights in an effort to efface their differences. It was not the same Warren who, the next morning, might tell Ed that he had no balls. Nor the same Warren who, the day after that, might tell Ed that he was the brightest person he'd ever met. He was sincere in these contradictions. He saw through people, but he also saw through himself, and this did not leave him sour or disdainful but amused, happily jaded. He had a mildness in his eyes that said, I know something you will never know. Once you saw that look, you didn't stop thinking about it.

The Peach Bowl took place in Atlanta, at Grant Field, on the campus of Georgia Tech. It was ASU's first national bowl game, the climax of their 10–0 season under longtime coach Frank

Kush. It was one of those back-and-forth games that inflames the emotions, as if the outcome were personal and spoke to your judgment, your taste, your capabilities. On their first possesssion, ASU marched seventy-eight yards downfield in only nine plays, ending in a touchdown run by their star back, Bob Thomas, who shimmered through the North Carolina defense like light on the surface of a pool. By the beginning of the second quarter, the Sun Devils were ahead 14–0, but then everything fell apart—a fumble, an intercepted pass—the kind of self-inflicted failure that bears the moral stigma of fecklessness, apathy, laziness. Suddenly North Carolina was ahead and it was halftime. The freezing rain that had made it uncomfortable to sit in the stands all afternoon now changed to heavy snow. "This does not count as a vacation," Susie said in the line for the restroom, holding a cup of hot coffee. Ed laughed and put his arm around her, slapping her jacketed elbow, and everyone smiled, but they also looked down at the ground. The weather was going to hurt ASU, not North Carolina. ASU relied on speed, and the snow would hobble them. You began to feel a little foolish for not anticipating the loss. With their orange-and-yellow uniforms, with the jauntiness of their nickname, the Sun Devils suddenly appeared like brash newcomers, cursed by a lack of history. They were only talented, nothing else.

But instead of losing, they won. They racked up three touchdowns and two field goals in the second half—they seemed to do nothing but score in the second half. They trounced North Carolina by twenty-two points. When the polls came out the next week, they stood a good chance of ranking number one.

Two weeks later, Ed and Warren filed the articles of incorporation for their new business, Consolidated Acceptance Corporation.

October 4, 1971. The day after they made their trip to Verde
Lakes and Chino Meadows, Ed drove Harry Gillis to the Scottsdale airport. Jack Ross met them inside the tiny terminal with
its vending machines selling coffee and sandwiches on rotating
disks. Ross, the brother of Goldwater's son-in-law, was a tall, bois-
terous crank with a brown mustache and glasses with thick frames
made of black plastic. He shook your hand too hard, slapped
your back. He seemed like a man playing a mayor in an amateur
stage play.

"You're not coming with us?" he asked Ed. "Can't get you up
there?"

"Not today."

"Really."

"No. I wish, but I've got work to do."

Gillis flicked his cigarette at one of the standing ashtrays.
"What kind of plane do you have?" he asked Ross, who clasped
his hands behind his waist and looked out at the runway, his chin
tucked in until it doubled.

"Aero Commander," he said. "Six-eighty."

"That's a Douglas?"

"Aero Design. Used to be Douglas, then they formed
their own outfit. Nice five-passenger plane. Single-engine prop
plane."

Through the airport's high windows, you could see the asphalt
lanes on the dried-out beige clay of the tarmac. Ed left them there
talking about engines. That was the last moment anyone would
be able to agree about. After that, everyone would have his own
story about what went wrong.

An accumulation of statements. A flood of documents, a five-year barrage.

On October 4, 1971, Jack Ross thinks to write a "personal memorandum" recounting his flight that day over Chino Grande with Harry Gillis of CMS, Japan. Ross thinks to paraphrase Gillis describing himself as "a professional land acquisition specialist and real estate person." He thinks to mention that Gillis declined an offer to also view the property from the ground—an important claim. Perhaps all of this happened as Ross said it did. Perhaps Jack Ross always wrote such detailed memoranda of his days.

On September 28, 1972, Harry Gillis gives a deposition in which he says it was Ned Warren's idea—not his or Ross's—that they view the property by plane, as opposed to from the ground. He says that previously, in Japan, Warren presented photographs of what he said was Chino Grande, which Warren described as "meadow"—gently rolling acreage easily divisible into five-acre rectangular parcels. A lawyer asks Gillis if he ever in fact actually saw the Chino Grande property.

"That is a good question, isn't it?" Gillis answers. "I was told I did."

And yet on the flight with Jack Ross, Gillis says, he didn't see any cliffs or canyons, did not observe a craggy landscape that could in no way be divided into neat, rectangular, five-acre parcels.

．　　．　　．

On June 16, 1972, Warren writes to his attorney, Philip Goldstein, to explain that subdividing the land into five-acre parcels had not been his responsibility, but rather the Japanese company CMS's. He writes: "The Arizona Real Estate Department is completely aware of the fact that we sold 40 acre parcels only. I visited the Real Estate Department and spoke with Mr. Talley and Mr. Kieffer. They both told me to advise CMS not to sell five acre parcels without receiving subdivision approval. That day I telephoned CMS and so advised them. They continued to sell five acre parcels after my warning."

On September 28, 1972, Harry Sperber of CMS, Japan, gives a deposition about how he learned of the subdivision status of Chino Grande, Arizona: "I asked him [James Kieffer, chief investigator, Arizona department of real estate] if this was true, if this was an illegal subdivision. And he then went on to explain that it was, that they didn't have a record of the plat, and they had complaints from a few of our clients. And I asked him what he thought, you know, could be done."

Sperber then recalls a lunch they had that day, which began with Warren greeting the CMS representatives at the bar with the words, "Are you guys going to sue me?"

Sperber's boss, Robert Kaplan, had answered, "Look, we ain't here to sue anybody. We just want to straighten this problem out."

"Well, if you sue me, I'll deny anything you say," Warren had responded. Then they had lunch.

On December 6, 1974, Jack Ross's lawyer, Jack McCormick, describes to Ross in a letter a conversation he's just had with a former CMS executive named Dale Hunt. Dale Hunt, McCormick writes, said that CMS was "fully aware" that Chino Grande was not a qualified subdivision when they began selling lots in Japan. According to Hunt, CMS was also "in some difficulty" with American military authorities over other land deals. Hunt acknowledged that CMS had had "an opportunity to inspect the property to any extent they deemed necessary" and that "their inspection was, nonetheless, inadequate."

On March 27, 1972, Robert Gunnison of Consolidated Acceptance Corporation gives a deposition about why Chino Grande could never be granted subdivision approval: "Five-acre parcels would require health department approval at both the county and the state level. The county would turn us down because most of the terrain is rock and there would be no percolation for septic tank use.…The state would turn us down because of the slope and angles of the lots…because of the rock and steep slopes, cliffs, road construction would be impossible in most of the area."

About a year later, on June 8, 1973, Warren is asked in a deposition how he could have gone to Japan and described such land as gentle, rolling meadows. He responds, "Apparently it was not as represented to me and as I represented it to CMS."

"How did the discrepancy come about?"

"I don't know."

On September 28, 1972, Robert Kaplan of CMS gives a deposition about Ned Warren's sales pitch the previous year in Japan. "As a matter of fact, he even brought a letter from Senator Goldwater when I saw him the next time." Kaplan recalls that the letter was "a great help in our selling program." He adds, of Warren, "It looked like we were really dealing with a reputable guy."

On September 9, 1976, he recounts his first trip to Chino Grande and says that the land looked "like goat's country. Would go up two, three hundred feet, then it would come down sheer.

"We always hoped there was something we could do, that we could straighten up the land, that we could carve it up. I'm telling you, when I saw that land, there was no way."

On October 19, 1976, Barry Goldwater issues a press statement saying he has been "unable to determine who among his friends asked him to write a laudatory letter that was used to promote a Ned Warren Sr. land-sales operation among U.S. servicemen in the Far East." The letter, as far as Goldwater knew at the time, referred to a Consolidated Mortgage subdivision called Chino Valley, near Prescott. It did not refer to the land near Seligman known as Chino Grande.

———————

The FBI file on Chino Grande is three inches thick—I have another inch of depositions and court exhibits. A patch of desert was viewed from Jack Ross's airplane by CMS's Harry Gillis. After that, all that can be done is to triangulate the various evasions. I think it's almost certain that my father never saw the land at Chino Grande—"goat's country," "cliffs." It was a side deal in a larger deal, it happened quickly, he was in Arizona when Warren made his trip to Japan. My father's own statements are vague, minimal. It's as if for a few months in 1971 he was just lazy, or careless, but of course laziness and carelessness are not characteristics that anyone speaks of when describing my father.

What ends up being called greed doesn't look like greed, it looks like giving things a go, seizing the main chance.

9

onzo McCracken was the senior detective in the Intelligence Division of the Phoenix police, the division that handled organized crime. He had a lined face, a straight, nearly lipless mouth, and guarded, close-set eyes. His work gave him ulcers, or aggravated them. He wrote memos for his personal record—obsessive, crammed with detail, each fact locked in his mind to twelve or fifteen others.

> To be concerned is enough to rip your guts out. The alternative, disregard it and go on—, become a part of it by your silence. At times the sins of omission are greater than the sins of commission. This would be brought home with devistating [*sic*] clarity if you were to sit in my office and watch an older man and his wife crying because their life savings from the sale of their home, their farm, was gone, all that was left represented in a stack of worthless documents. To ignore the problem any longer, I feel would be dereliction of duty.

About three months after James Cornwall became president of the Great Southwest Land and Cattle Company—in January 1971—McCracken and his partner, Bill Bouley, drove to an office on East Camelback Road, not far from the offices of Consolidated Mortgage Corporation, to speak to an informant named Tony Serra. Tony Serra was the lot salesman at ALCO who had helped Warren manufacture land contracts to sell through Diamond Valley, the company Warren later sold off to Lee Ackerman. Serra had also been a sales manager for James Cornwall at Great Southwest. More recently, he had started his own business, Western World Development, to sell Great Southwest land and paper in the manner Warren had taught him.

The office of Western World looked more like the back room of a store: a few plastic chairs against a bare wall, a calendar from an auto parts wholesaler, a carpet remnant on the linoleum floor, a card table with three newspapers from the previous month. The girl behind the desk wore a crochet dress and had long, straight hair and hoop earrings. She did not end her phone conversation, even when McCracken took off his jacket, revealing his holstered gun. She parted her lips a little, half looking, half concentrating on the voice on the line.

"No one's in yet," she said, her hand covering the receiver. "You could try back in half an hour."

"It's ten o'clock," McCracken said. "Our appointment was for nine-thirty."

"Then they must be late. They're usually here by ten."

Bouley stood with his feet apart, hands in a bridge before his waist. McCracken nodded his head, looking at the floor.

"Tell Mr. Serra we'll be waiting for him at the coffee shop across the street," he said. "The Pullman Pie, it's called."

. . .

They sat in a booth near the window and had coffee.

"Serra's not really anybody," McCracken said. "He knows a few of the Ivanhoe crowd. Talks a lot."

"He's from Cleveland?" asked Bouley.

"St. Louis. He was in the insurance racket there. I don't know what else he got up to."

A car pulled into the parking lot—a deliberately Hollywood entrance, complete with squealing tires and a sudden, juddering stop at an angle to the parking lines. The car was a white Rolls-Royce Silver Shadow. McCracken thought, this is how people get killed, by sitting in a coffee shop that turns out to be the imagined set of somebody else's action movie. He watched the driver step out, a stocky white-haired man in a tan leisure suit. The man stood up straight and jammed a pistol into his waistband. He made sure the gesture was as visible as possible. Then another man got out of the backseat, Tony Serra.

McCracken took a sip of his coffee. When he looked up again, he saw the driver open the restaurant's glass door with a jangle of bells, Serra behind him, already scanning the tables. He wore a charcoal suit and a shiny green tie with scarlet stripes. When he saw McCracken, his face looked absent. Then he recognized him. He put his hand on the driver's shoulder and turned his head back toward the door, indicating that he should leave.

He apologized, standing at their booth. He explained that the girl at the desk had forgotten to mention that McCracken and Bouley were detectives—all she'd said was that two men with guns had come by.

"It's all right," McCracken said, barely looking at Serra. "I guess her talent is more for answering phones."

Serra sat down and ordered a coffee. McCracken took out his notebook and pen and on the next blank page wrote a dateline with Serra's source ID. The waitress brought over the coffee pot and poured into Serra's cup, then refilled McCracken's and Bouley's. McCracken looked at his watch and wrote down the time. They talked for about half an hour.

"Cornwall," Serra said toward the end. "He's the one you want to look at first."

"The southerner," said McCracken.

"He seems like a southerner. Actually he's from some cracker town in Oregon. Dig around, you'll find his signature on twenty, thirty loans—loans to pay off loans. More than a million dollars, maybe more like five."

McCracken flipped back a few pages in his notebook to an earlier part of their conversation. He had written the words NED WARREN and then a scribble of details. Everyone in the land business, Serra had told him, knew that Ned Warren was behind more than a dozen companies in one way or another. He said that the Mafia's biggest interest in Arizona at that point was not gambling, not prostitution, not loan-sharking, but the land business. That's why they'd sent him there from St. Louis ten years ago, Serra said, to find a way into the land business.

Serra saw from across the table the notation about Warren in McCracken's book. "You're going to have a hard time getting anywhere with this," he said.

"Why's that?"

"Because—you know how this town is. Warren, those people, they've got everyone tied in."

"Who's everyone?"

"Everyone. The real estate commissioner, Talley. All his investigators. They've got the county prosecutor, the attorney general. They've probably got Barry Goldwater."

McCracken paid for the three coffees. Some parts of the story seemed more or less credible, but it was all coming from Tony Serra—the expensive new suit, the fantasist with the breath mints and cologne. At first, McCracken didn't take it very seriously.

It was almost a year after that conversation—the first week of December 1971—that the complaints began to arrive from Japan. A few servicemen had paid for their lots in cash rather than in installments. They went looking for their titles and deeds, only to find out that no titles or deeds existed. Chino Grande did not exist in any legal sense. Ed was staring fixedly at the pen resting at a slant on his desk.

"Are they still selling over there?" he asked Warren over the phone.

"Well, they'd better not be selling five-acre parcels."

"I guess I'm wondering, what did you tell them?"

"We'll get this fixed. They'll have to get a subdivision approved, but that shouldn't take long. Talley's on it. He's got the heat on Japan, not on us."

"Where is Ross in all this?"

"Ross doesn't want to hear a word about it."

"Did he say it was a subdivision or not?"

"If Ross needs a subdivision approved, he'll get a subdivision approved. Who do you think got us that letter from Goldwater?"

They hung up. They had close relations with the Real Estate Department. Chino Meadows had been approved in a single day, without anyone even viewing the property. At that point, no one but Ross had actually seen the land at Chino Grande. Ed thought of Talley in his double-knit shirt, of Ross in his white belt, and he told himself that none of this could be very serious. It didn't seem serious until he went through the ledger and began paying the bills for that month.

In the large stack of checks prepared for his authorization each month, there would always be one made out for $200 to one of Warren's corporations—Camelback Mortgage, WR Investments, Pacific West Realty—there were several. The checks were prepared by the office manager, Warren's ex-mistress Donna Stevens, who entered the payments into the Consolidated ledger as broker's fees. Donna Stevens had set up the ledger herself before Ed had even started at Consolidated, and she had inserted a separate card as a reminder each month to write the check. The recipient companies, rotated by her like specials on a menu, were all controlled by Warren, who had Donna, an officer in all these companies, cash the checks and then deliver the money to him in an envelope. In the business world in Phoenix, it was expected that you would get into a little trouble from time to time, that you would need a favor—that was how business worked, through favors. You would need to approach the men in charge of water rights in Prescott, for example, or the men at the Energy Department who installed gas lines, or the men at the Forest Service who could grant you an easement or a rezoning if you suddenly needed more land. You would buy them a case of Scotch, or take them for a round of golf. People who didn't smile at this kind of arrangement had no sense of lightness, no sense of humor—they didn't even quite understand that these things went on. Warren didn't have to explain this to Ed. Ed could see right away that saying anything about the checks would only make him look hapless.

The $200 payment had started out as "money well spent," in Warren's words—bonuses for the salesmen, charitable donations, campaign contributions. But after a few months in the business—the monthly check always for the same amount—Ed knew enough to know that this particular $200 was in fact not casual but a regular payment to the real estate commissioner, J. Fred Talley, who got the same payment from every land company in Arizona. He made almost $10,000 a month in this way. It had seemed a little ugly to Ed, primitive, but it had also seemed like a formality, a gesture of obeisance, like getting your real estate license. He was playing the game basically straight, straighter than almost anyone else, and it was only now, with the first complaints about Chino Grande arriving from Japan, that he saw the monthly payments as something more serious. He saw that from any objective point of view they would simply look like bribes.

He put the checks in a rubber band and then he put his pen in its holder, his papers in a neat stack on the side of his desk. Then he picked up the duffel bag in which he kept his tennis clothes—if you left them in the car, they got too hot to wear—and went out to the secretaries with the bag and his mail in two clipped bundles, interoffice and postal.

"What time did Elaine come in this morning?" he asked Sharon, stern, his brow coming down at her like that of a bird of prey.

"She was here early," Sharon said. "She was here at eight-thirty, I think. Why?"

Ed shook his head. "I doubt that very much." He sighed. "Get your things together. You're fired. Get out."

Sharon's face went blank.

"They just waltz in here," Ed said, leaning over her desk. "They waltz in and they think you'll cover for them. Is that the way it is?"

He didn't know why he was doing this. It took Sharon a long time to realize he was only joking. She tried to smile then, her eyes a little wet. "That isn't funny," she said.

He brushed her on the shoulder, tilting his head at her skeptically. "Come on."

She wouldn't smile. He placed the mail on her desk and left.

The Jewish Community Center. Two men playing tennis on their lunch hour, white shirts and white shorts. This was the person he was, the ball a yellow blur over the net, no thought but the thought of the motion. The deep *pock* sound of the ground strokes. The hesitation before the ball toss, the long inhale, the smooth rise of the racket up the back, past the shoulder blade, the sudden overhead slam. The game in endless deuce—first serve, second serve. Afterward, the shower, the thick white towels, a sandwich and an iced tea on the deck.

He played with Barry Starr that day. Barry Starr could not have known what was going on in his mind.

That afternoon, Warren came into the office in a brown suit with his briefcase. He had Sharon bring him in a coffee with cream and two sugars.

"Cornwall says he wants to keep his override," he said.

Ed nodded, poker-faced. Great Southwest was in such trouble by now that Consolidated Acceptance was managing some of its sales, helping it scratch out a profit on its newly acquired subdivision near Casa Grande. Even now, Cornwall refused to take a pay cut, nor did Warren insist that he do so.

"Where's he going to find the money to pay himself?" Ed asked.

"I told him the same thing. I told him it would be Chapter Eleven if he keeps it up, but he doesn't listen."

Ed pushed a folder toward Warren. There was only so much of his bluff you could resist before the struggle made you feel ridiculous. "We'll sell his lots on our contracts, not Great Southwest's," he said. "They pay the up-front costs, the promotion. They give us fifty percent of the down, then fifteen of the flow. If it works, fine. If it doesn't, we're through with them. I assume you've been pulling your money out all this time."

Warren sipped his coffee. He pretended to contemplate the folder but didn't even open it up. "I'm going over to see Talley now," he said. "I'm going to talk to him some more about this Chino Grande deal, the subdivision approval. What we can do to make this work. I think you should come along."

Ed was silent for a moment. Warren wasn't looking at him, and Ed sat there with his fingers on his chin, watching Warren's face as he looked down at the folder. First there was the line about Great Southwest—*I told him the same thing. I told him it would be Chapter Eleven if he keeps it up*—as if the bankruptcy weren't a likely possibility, as if Warren weren't instigating it. Now there was this prod to go watch him hand Talley the envelope full of cash.

"I'm not doing that," he said.

Warren tapped the folder. "You sounded very concerned about Chino Grande on the phone before, that's all."

"I am concerned."

Warren took a long sip of his coffee. He squinted, running his tongue along his upper lip. "I don't like it any more than you do that we're tied in with these people," he said. "Cornwall. Ross. They're the ones that should be bearing the brunt of their own mistakes. We've been running this business for two years, and we've always been straight. I've always been able to say, look, we're doing it by the book, we're clean—I told it to Don Bolles at the *Republic*, I told him to write a story about it. That's what matters to me, that we've always been clean. So you see what's at stake right now. Not just Ross but Cornwall—this whole shadow starting to hang over us. You see what's at stake, not just for me but for you."

Ed shook his head. "I'm not going."

Warren nodded. He turned at the waist, as if looking for Sharon to come take away his coffee cup, and in that one movement his whole demeanor seemed to change. There was the briefest glimpse of contempt, and then there was self-possession. You could see that he was going to be mild, even cheerful, but absolutely silent about whatever he was thinking. It was suddenly as though the whole conversation had not occurred.

He stood up and patted Ed on the shoulder. "Okay," he said. "No hard feelings, then."

Ed nodded, shaking his hand.

"I'll see you later," Warren said.

Things were never the same.

10

I was looking just a few weeks ago for some more information about American Home Industries, the company that bought Consolidated Mortgage from my father and Warren in 1971, and then later, in 1972, filed for bankruptcy. I had done an Internet search earlier, typing in "American Home Industries," but the name is general and nothing useful came up. They become compulsive, though, these searches, so a few weeks ago, I tried out some variations and it was there—the company was still there. One of the names listed was familiar. I knew the name because I know all these names now. I know them the way I know my phone number and address.

I called the number on the site without even preparing any questions. I knew better than this, but I did it because at that moment it felt like it was 1972 and not 2007. It felt like I could get the story in this one phone call, a ridiculous feeling I have had several times throughout this project, always immediately refuted.

The voice at the other end of the line was deep and assertive, but also guarded, the voice, I imagined, of someone who had made and lost money, a business voice. He recognized my last name.

Perhaps that was why he took my call. The more we talked, the more his voice reminded me of another voice I had heard while doing this research. I had discovered, through a complicated set of circumstances, a few taped interviews made by journalists in Arizona in 1976, among them an interview with David Rich, who is now dead but who spoke at length back then about my father. That was how I learned that David Rich had an English accent. I heard him speaking on tape about my father's story, and the sound of Rich's voice made the story seem more real, that is to say smaller, less mythic. There was another taped interview with a man named A. A. McCollum, whose voice sounded like the man from American Home Industries. A. A. McCollum bought Consolidated Mortgage in 1973, after Consolidated had separated from AHI. By 1973, Consolidated's assets had been compromised, and McCollum lost everything. His voice on tape had a certain flatness you hear in California, an accent perhaps transplanted there from the Midwest. It was the same timbre I heard in the voice of the man I talked to now, the man from American Home Industries.

What happened, as the man explained it to me, was that the housing market began to collapse in 1972. The Vietnam War, the rising cost of oil—it was the beginning of what would come to be known as *stagflation*, the deep recession that would eventually characterize the whole decade. The Fed raised interest rates. Almost immediately, no one could get the financing to build houses. AHI's stock was traded on the NASDAQ, so all you had to do was look at the morning paper to see how far it had fallen.

The man told me something he'd never told anyone then, not even his wife. On the stroke of midnight one night, the phone rang, and it was Ned Warren calling from Phoenix. Warren said he wanted out of the merger with AHI, he wanted his Consolidated stock back. The man didn't want to tell me exactly what Warren said after that. He told me that the next time he met Warren, in Phoenix, he brought along an associate who was carrying a .45 beneath his jacket. My father was at that meeting. I asked the man what my father was like and he said that he didn't talk a lot, he was the quiet one, very much the accountant. It was Warren who made all the decisions.

I asked him if Warren had threatened his life the night of that midnight phone call, but he was not comfortable giving me any more details. It had been thirty-five years. Eventually we talked again, and he told me that for a long time in that period he'd had to park his car in a different spot every day. He said that he never drove without first checking underneath the car for what might be there.

PART THREE

"This is going to be very confusing. It's confusing in my own mind."

—Ed Lazar before the grand jury,
January 9, 1975

II

New Year's Day 1972. They were at the Biltmore Hotel, with its wide lawns under Squaw Peak, having brunch with their wives. There was the gilt ceiling, the pianist playing jazz, the prime rib under its red lamp. On the patio outside, Warren stood against a pillar made of concrete blocks carved to resemble the trunk of a palm tree. He lit a cigarette, his khaki suit seeming to rebuff the sunlight. Ed sat in a deck chair and looked down into his glass of Scotch. Before them both was the Olympic-size pool—the neat ranks of empty chaises longues, the high dive—the pool that had once been Marilyn Monroe's favorite pool in the world.

"That was the right thing to do, not going to Talley's," Warren said. "Those things are always a gray area. When to help, when not to. When to keep your distance."

Ed turned the glass in his hand, feeling the moisture bleed through the tufted cocktail napkins. Since their dispute, Warren had been neither hostile nor affable, just industrious, sending Ed memos and specs about sites in Arizona, Utah, Oklahoma, Oregon—land everywhere, executives he'd met through the network. They had barely spoken about Talley or Ross or CMS. They had just gone deeper into the fray of business. On paper, they were still worth $5 million.

"You said you had some news about Oklahoma," Ed said, changing the subject. "Why don't you tell me about that?"

"It's beautiful land." Warren put away his lighter, raising his eyebrows. "It's like Verde, only there's more of it. Green, mountains, not hot. We can go up there and look at it sometime. Meanwhile, there's something under way here. Very high-end land, just north of town, it's called the Rose Garden. As in 'Rosenzweig.' "

Ed squinted. "Harry Rosenzweig?"

"We have lunch together once in a while, a drink. Harry had some stock we helped him with—ten thousand or so, it was in his wife's name. This was that Educational Computer deal. You remember that? When we merged Great Southwest with Educational Computer?"

"Harry Rosenzweig."

"Some of that stock was Harry Rosenzweig's."

Harry Rosenzweig happened to be there that morning, seated near the piano, surrounded, as he always was, by a crowd. Ed had seen him as he and Warren left for the patio, a man with white hair and sideburns, a deep tan, the avid gaze of some figure you might spot at Palm Springs or Las Vegas. He was Barry Goldwater's oldest boyhood friend. He had managed Goldwater's presidential campaign in '64, had been a longtime chairman of the Arizona Republican Party. If you read the newspaper in Phoenix, then you knew that in some mysterious way Harry Rosenzweig ran the city. He did not hold office, but placed people there—the county prosecutor, the police chief, the city council, the board of supervisors. They were there because Harry wanted or allowed them to be there. Every public official in Phoenix began his career with a visit to Rosenzweig's Jewelers, where Harry had his office on the second floor, overlooking the showroom with its glass cases.

"You remember those people at Fuqua?" Warren asked, looking at Ed.

"No. Fuqua?"

"Fuqua Industries. Out in San Diego. Another one of those deals I'm in with Dave Rich."

Ed didn't smile, but he had to resist the urge. They still liked each other—that was something he could not deny, even now. David Rich, Harry Rosenzweig, Fuqua, the Rose Garden: Warren explained the whole knotted story, not slowly, not patiently, just putting it out there in hard, clean shapes. They had known each other for fifteen, twenty years, Dave and Harry, had bought some land together called the Rose Garden. Now Warren was going to help them sell it at a good price to a conglomerate called Fuqua Industries in San Diego. If Ed wanted to join them as broker, he could take away about $50,000 for half an hour of having drinks with everyone. It would be a way of making it up to him for all the trouble with Jack Ross and CMS.

New Year's Day. Sunlight on the blue sky, the purple rock of the peak, people playing golf in midwinter. On the patio, after a few drinks, the Chino Grande deal seemed far away, a minor stumble amid a dozen deals, $100,000 tied up in escrow.

"Harry Rosenzweig," Ed said.

Warren blew out smoke. "Why don't we go inside and I'll introduce you."

They went back into the dining room, past the tables with their white cloths, the ice sculpture on its silver platform. *You have to realize that Ned is Ned*, Barbara Warren had whispered earlier, her hand on Ed's hand, confiding. *Ned's a piece of work, but he always lands on his feet. Always.* Now Warren clasped his hands behind his waist as he moved through the room. Ed followed, leaving his napkin-wrapped drink on someone's half-cleared table. He watched as Warren put his hand on Harry Rosenzweig's shoulder and Rosenzweig cocked his head a little to better concentrate on what Warren was telling him.

"One of my stand-outs," Warren said. "One of the brightest young men around, Ed Lazar. He works with me over at Consolidated Mortgage."

Rosenzweig looked up at Ed with the delight of someone whose expectations of people had not diminished since childhood. There was the impeccably cut white hair, the mild cologne. You couldn't help feeling magnified by his attention, reassured by the dryness and warmth of Harry Rosenzweig's hand.

Harry Rosenzweig

The years of his early family life—happy, especially happy in hindsight. A son and a daughter, almost four and almost two, Zachary and Stacey. A ranch house full of noise, laundry, the cleaning woman on Wednesdays, Susie tired, needing a vacation. Ed faded in and out sometimes, thirty-eight years old but feeling now that thirty-eight was hardly old at all, even forty was hardly old at all. He would leave the office for a few hours in the afternoons, go for a drive, not telling anyone where, just disappearing. At night, he and Ron Fineberg still went out for drinks. Ed "could sweet-talk any beautiful woman," Ron would say later. He was not a talker but he had the smile, could flirt without saying very much, letting the silence or a few simple words cast everything in a comic, uncertain, suggestive light. He slipped in and out of moments, all of them real but transient, floating, maybe a little boring if he stayed too long.

To be not just eager, talented, "bright"—instead, to be poised. There was something compelling about Warren, even now, because Ed could see the limitations of his own scruples. The scruples could seem fussy, weak, collegiate. At times, they seemed to constitute a kind of failure.

Blackbrush, shadscale, greasewood. Dark land under clouds— borax, potash, salt. A sudden rain washed down cliffs. Flood pools formed, flood pools dried out. A sequence of events unfolded without witnesses, without meaning.

At Durant's restaurant, you parked in the back and went in through the kitchen, past the line cooks, the waiters hustling by in their half tuxedos. They carried trays of large white plates covered by lank sirloins, chops, strip steaks, potato on the side with a thick slice of buttered toast. Ed and Warren had just made a down payment on two thousand acres in Oklahoma and now CMS had come to discuss what could be done with the Jack Ross acreage at Chino Grande. Ed had arrived late, so he wasn't at the bar when Warren had first joined up with CMS's Robert Kaplan and Harry Sperber, there in place of Harry Gillis. They were all sitting at the table now with their menus and drinks. James Kieffer of the Real Estate Department was also there, a man in his thirties with slicked-back hair and sideburns that cut down across his cheeks. He was Talley's chief investigator. He had just broken the news that Chino Grande was not a legal subdivision, that there was in fact no such thing as Chino Grande. He looked impotent and stern, sitting upright in his plaid sport coat, a clerk with a blotched face, a salary in the low teens.

"I told him we're not here to sue anybody," Kaplan told Ed before Ed even sat down. "We want to work something out, that's all."

Ed put a *Time* magazine down on the table. On the cover was Liza Minnelli in a black hat, a black leotard, mascara. "Well, that's good you're not going to sue," he said. "That would make for an awkward lunch."

No one laughed. They had just been through this already, and Warren had bluntly told them that if they sued he would just deny everything.

"I spoke to Ross," Kieffer said. "He said to call his lawyer. That was all he had to say."

"I'm not surprised," Ed said a little sarcastically. "Did he offer to show you around in his plane?"

"I'm just trying to clear this up."

"I understand. The fact is he won't talk to us either."

Kieffer was sitting next to Warren, who was eyeing the magazine cover.

"'The New Miss Show Biz,'" he said. "I don't understand the appeal of Liza Minnelli."

"She looks like a boy," suggested Kaplan.

"I see," Warren said. "Though not really."

Their booth curved around three sides of the table, so no one's back was to the room. There were white tablecloths, red wallpaper embossed with silk, as in a bordello. Kieffer looked mistrustfully at his silverware, as if he were already anticipating the arrival of the check and his inability to pay his share. His presence aroused suspicion. The lunch went badly. The proposals Ed made—an exchange for lots in other subdivisions, a discount on the price—met with skeptical shrugs. *We're not here to sue anybody*, Kaplan had said. But what he really meant was there was no incentive for CMS to do anything but wait for their money back.

In the parking lot, Warren handed Ed a slip of paper, a tear-off form for telephone messages. It gave the date and time and the name of the caller: Detective Lonzo McCracken, Phoenix police.

James Kieffer stood watching beside Warren, perhaps more aware of what was happening than Ed was.

"Lonzo McCracken," Warren said to Ed. "Odd name. I'll have my lawyer call Mo Berger, the county prosecutor. See what he has to say about Lonzo McCracken."

Ed looked down at his car keys. "I don't want to be hearing this."

"That makes two of us," said Warren.

"What do you want from me?"

"I want you to not worry. I'll meet with this cop and I'll straighten him out. I'll have my lawyer call our friend Moise Berger. That will be that."

"Ross went to the police," Ed said.

"It wasn't Ross. You think Ross wants the police involved?"

"Then, who was it?"

"It's pretty obvious. It was Jim Cornwall."

Ed got into his car. He placed his briefcase and the *Time* magazine on the passenger seat and put his key in the ignition, not looking at anything but the dashboard, the steering wheel, the rearview mirror. Jim Cornwall. If Jim Cornwall was talking to the police, it meant that things were even worse than he'd realized. It meant that Great Southwest was facing not just bankruptcy but criminal charges. It meant that Warren's life was about to be scrutinized by the police, and by extension so was his own.

Every time he'd made a payment to Talley, he had strengthened his resemblance to James Cornwall. Every payment of his to Talley had been matched by a similar payment from Cornwall, channeled through the same chain of Warren-controlled corporations. Every payment to Talley had made it more difficult to argue that there was any real difference between Consolidated Mortgage and Great Southwest, between himself and James Cornwall.

I'll have my lawyer call Mo Berger, the county prosecutor.

Our friend Moise Berger.

12

The office smelled like air freshener, beneath the scent the faint sourness of cigarettes. Warren started to hand the envelope across his desk, then drew it back, smiling, as if to say maybe the photographs were inside, maybe they weren't. Maybe it didn't matter. Probably if he had the photographs he wouldn't be passing them over his desk in the middle of the afternoon, as a kind of joke, to the county prosecutor's own investigator, George Brooks. But perhaps the mere rumor of their existence would be enough to keep Moise Berger in their circle.

I'll have my lawyer call Mo Berger, the county prosecutor.

Our friend Moise Berger.

"I would say you're joking, but I know you're not," George Brooks said, sitting in his chair with crossed legs.

Warren put the envelope back on his desk. "Berger doesn't seem like the type," he said.

"Everyone's the type. But Berger's always been clean. Seersucker suit, white bucks. He used to come to work with his lunch in his briefcase, like his wife made it for him every morning. Harry Rosenzweig's bright young star."

"He can't handle his liquor, I guess."

"Which I didn't think he even drank." Brooks looked down at his fingers. "Who's the girl?"

Warren just shook his head. "What I'm telling you is that I wouldn't worry about Moise Berger anymore. You can take the money from Cornwall and wave it right in Berger's face if you want."

"It's one of Harry Rosenzweig's girls?"

"Take the two thousand and buy yourself a cabin in the woods. I don't know anything about Harry Rosenzweig's girls."

Brooks squinted, meeting Warren's gaze, then looked out the office window. They had known each other for almost ten years, Warren and Brooks. They had known each other from Brooks's days working as Talley's investigator—the job James Kieffer held now—back when Brooks was first learning how the land business operated. The idea that Warren might have compromising photographs of Moise Berger did not come as a surprise to George Brooks.

George Brooks: Moise Berger.

James Kieffer: J. Fred Talley.

George Brooks is to Moise Berger as James Kieffer is to J. Fred Talley.

A $2,000 loan to George Brooks, another $2,600 loan to James Kieffer.

This is going to be very confusing. It's confusing in my own mind.

———

"I received a check from CONSOLIDATED MORTGAGE in the amount of $250" [Louis Lazar said]. "$50 was to be for my income tax...." He then deposited the CMC check in his L & B REALTY account and wrote out another check:

"I made this check out to myself in the amount of $200.... I cashed it.... Took the $200, I gave it to NED WARREN.... Probably the same date, I generally cashed it and gave it to him the same day.... Gave it to him in his office on Central Avenue off Osborn.... Generally an office girl was there.... I'd walk in the office and the girl was in front and I'd say, 'I'd like to see MR. WARREN,' and she'd—I usually would walk right in there and give it to him...."

> Q: *And did he say anything at the time that he took the money?*
> A: *Nothing.*

—from a deposition given by my grandfather,
Louis Lazar, July 15, 1975

Four days passed after the meeting with CMS and Kieffer. For four days, Ed didn't sleep, stirring at two or three with a dry mouth, then failing to concentrate on a book under the living room lamp. This was how it would be when he was old, he thought: insomnia, roiling anxiety, the body and mind at odds with each other, or rather, in mutually destructive accord.

He had signed a personal guarantee on the loan for the land in Oklahoma—two thousand acres bought on credit. He owed more money now than he could pay back anytime soon. There would be no easy way to walk away from the business, even if he wanted to, and he didn't know what he would do instead—ask for his old job back at Gallant, Farrow?

That Friday was the Sabbath, so they went as usual to his parents' for dinner. His parents were small, compact, Lou about five foot five, Belle not even five feet, though always in high heels. They were children of Romanian immigrants, neither of them certain of their actual date of birth. There was plastic fruit in bowls, wax fruit in bowls, plastic film on the sofa to protect its yellow upholstery. The house could seem almost holy in its lack of artifice. A glazed chicken baked in the double oven, and Ed and his father watched TV in a small room with matching recliners, a nightstand used as an end table, atop it a lamp and a pair of reading glasses and a crossword dictionary. It was close to tax season, so there were ways for Ed to present what he had to say to his father that would be predictably confusing, not suspiciously confusing, not that far out of the ordinary, but he couldn't bring himself to say it. They watched Bill Close, the anchorman, deliver an editorial on Richard Nixon's trip to China, behind Close a shot of Nixon and his wife, Pat, waving on the tarmac, returned home. It had been a historic trip, though the editorial did not make it clear why. It only made Nixon appear monumental.

"It looks like he'll get reelected," Ed said.

"He's the incumbent."

"The devil you know."

His father fingered a bowl of mixed nuts. Ed sat there looking at his own hand on the armrest of the recliner. Of all the things he did in these years, what he did that night would cause him the most shame.

I thought about this for a long time. I sat up several nights, asking myself if I had understood this properly. I thought about it for a long time because I had to explain to myself why my father had enlisted his own father in helping him bribe Talley with $200 that week, the same week that my father and Warren and James Cornwall loaned Talley's assistant, James Kieffer, $2,600.

———————

"I'm worried that Kieffer is a loose cannon," Warren had said to Ed that morning in the conference room. He'd looked bleary with activity, downshifting from business to the low realm of the Real Estate Department. James Kieffer, he explained, was bitter, frustrated—everything about the land business had started to disgust him. He drove out to the empty subdivisions and confirmed that the bulldozers were in operation, that the salesmen were at least licensed, and if they weren't, that they were fired. Then he made his phone calls back to the lot buyers, who demanded their money back anyway, who didn't understand why everything was moving so slowly, who cursed him or threatened to sue. When he spoke about this to Talley, Talley just shrugged, because to Talley it was all a game. Kieffer wasn't stupid, Warren explained, and he knew that Talley was taking money on all sides.

Ed looked out the window of the office. He saw Kieffer's blotched face, the sideburns, the greased-back hair. He was like the aged version of the hoods in high school, threatening now not because of physical toughness but because of the resentment brought on everywhere by money.

"I have nothing to hide from Jim Kieffer," Ed said.

"There's a cop out there, Lonzo McCracken, who wants to drag our names through the mud," Warren said quietly. "That's how they play these things, through the newspapers. That way they don't need any facts."

"What does Kieffer want?"

Warren clasped shut his briefcase. His suit could have been ten years old or brand-new, one of three dozen conservative suits in muted colors. "You would be surprised the way a person like Jim Kieffer thinks," he said. "I got him to take out a loan. Twenty-six hundred dollars was all it took to make him happy."

Ed looked down at the windowsill. "You had him sign a note?"

"I had him sign a note," Warren said. "It's not just cash this way, it's not just a gift. It's a corporate note with his signature on it."

Ed's hand was still on the window frame. He looked out at the sunlight and pursed his lips as if he had bitten into something unexpectedly strong. In a way, it was a smile. It was a disgusted smile at his own innocence. It took him a moment to understand what Warren meant. There was a show of weakness, a show of qualms. In that moment, Warren became more of an adversary.

"He knows about Talley," Warren went on. "He knows about Talley and now he knows that Cornwall is talking to this cop, McCracken, telling him God knows what, and all Kieffer wanted was twenty-six hundred dollars. It's already done, I already gave him the money. I'm asking for your help. I don't want a bunch of people pulling their money out of the business just because they've heard some rumors, or read a story in a newspaper. Cornwall gave me thirteen hundred—that's half. All I'm asking from you is six hundred and fifty."

———

Sabbath dinner. A challah bread, a glass of Cutty Sark for the men, candles but no wine. There was noodle kugel with raisins, glazed chicken, green beans with sliced almonds. In a closet off the kitchen, with its footstool for the high cabinets, were two "For

Sale" signs painted with the words *L & B Realty:* L & B for Louis and Belle Lazar, their realty agency, more a hobby than a business. I remember the realty signs like another toy in a house full of toys. I remember a great deal about that house. My grandmother collected china dolls in different period costumes. There was one dressed as a Beefeater, one as Anne Boleyn in a purple gown with an extra finger on one of her hands. My grandfather loved sports and kept his cousin Billy's boxing gloves as a memento of him—Billy, a boxer in the army in World War II, a Jewish boxer. I have the gloves now in my own closet at home.

"It's nothing serious," Ed told Lou after dinner. "Just some nonsense with the new tax laws. We have to move some money around. The usual song and dance with the IRS."

His father wasn't looking at him. He was looking at the sealed envelope addressed to L & B Realty.

"Just cash the check and bring it to Ned's," Ed said. "He'll take care of it from there."

He willed the scene into normalcy by simply watching his father, not saying anything until the strangeness passed.

The show of weakness, the show of qualms. There was the way Ed had stood at the window, as if he couldn't look Warren in the eye. There was the concentration on his face as he considered what Warren really meant by the loan to Kieffer. He thought about it for a long time afterward. He thought about James Cornwall talking to McCracken and he thought about the impasse with CMS, about James Kieffer bringing the news that Chino Grande was an illegal subdivision.

It was $650. It was nothing. He saw that if he stood on principle, then everyone would have no choice but to turn against him—Warren, Cornwall, Kieffer, Talley, possibly several others he didn't even know about yet.

"I think you should wash your own money from now on," Warren had told him, when he'd finally capitulated. "I don't think you want my help with that anymore. I think it would be better for you if you handled the money for Talley on your own."

Lou Lazar left the bank with the envelope of cash and got back into his car. He put the $200 in the glove box and started the ignition

The author as a newborn with his father and grandfathers, Ervin Berman (left) and Louis Lazar (right)

and drove slowly to the office building on Central Avenue. It was Tuesday, March 7, 1972. He had never heard of J. Fred Talley, had no idea what the $200 was for. The office building had an elevator even though there were only three floors, and on floor three you could have been in a dental complex: a gray carpeted hallway with freshly painted graphic designs on the walls, windows hung on the inside with white venetian blinds and stenciled in black with the names of the businesses. When the secretary let Lou into Warren's office, Warren was on the phone. He didn't hang up, just raised his eyebrows, his hand over the receiver, and indicated that Lou could leave the envelope on the desk.

———

"Fence-posting." "Hanging paper." Selling land to a stranger who was using a false name, or selling the same land to two or three different people in different states. Manufacturing contracts and then retailing the mortgages to still another person through a chain of corporations. These were some of the procedures Lonzo McCracken had learned about in the past year from Tony Serra.

Congratulations on your investment program with Western World Development, official broker of the Great Southwest Land and Cattle Company.

In a volatile market, mortgage securities are your safest, smartest bet for the future.

Lots are going fast in our scenic Beaver Valley subdivision.

Mr. and Mrs. Craig from Hannibal, Missouri. Mr. and Mrs. LaMotte from Utica, New York. Mr. and Mrs. West from Burnsville, Minnesota. They'd been coming to McCracken's office for the past month or so with their paperwork in accordion files, their fear like resentment in their eyes, telling him the same story they had now recited three or four times to different, unhelpful officials. Two quarter-acre lots near Wilcox, no deed ever sent, just tax forms and a payment booklet. Eleven payments made, then the mortgage reassigned to something called the Bemis Corporation, then the news that there was no deed, not even a lot, or maybe there were three buyers for the same lot, all of them still responsible for the payments, the checks due each month to Bemis or First Bank of Michigan or Spectrum Enterprises or the Franklin Bank of Texas. McCracken would take down their statements on a carbon form. They had written letters, the buyers would tell him: to the land companies, to the Real Estate Department, to the attorney general, to HUD. Did they have copies of these letters? No, they had not thought to make copies of the letters.

James Cornwall sat in the coffee shop, looking annoyed by some mild physical pain. He wore a linen suit with a tie and matching pocket square. He had ordered the steak sandwich, but he wasn't eating it and it sat before him as if that had been his intention all along. "What did Serra tell you?" he asked.

McCracken lowered his gaze, then looked Cornwall in the eye. "He said he had permission to turn Warren in. That was the phrase he used. I guess he meant permission from who he works for."

Cornwall looked across the restaurant, his eyes steady, sightless, his mouth a little open. They had always joked that Serra was "mini-Mafia," but it had always been a joke.

McCracken opened his hand beside his plate. "I'm trying to help you," he said. "I need a copy of the books. That's the only way we can go forward."

"I can't do that. You know I can't do that."

"Then I'll get a warrant."

———

"I need to talk to you," Cornwall said, standing in the doorway of the bedroom with his suit jacket still on, his unknotted tie around his neck. His wife lay in bed with the ten o'clock news on. He had talked to McCracken again—she knew and didn't want to discuss it anymore. She scratched the back of her neck, watching President Nixon campaign.

"He said he wants a copy of the books," Cornwall said. "He needs proof. I told him I couldn't do it—if I did that, he'd have me in a corner."

She moved her hand as if to brush something off the blanket. "So then we're back where we started."

"I was thinking I'd like to get out of Phoenix," he said, clearing his throat. "I'd like us to move back to Eugene."

Her eyes reacted to the TV, squinting or flinching, then going blank again, her mind back on what they were discussing. "How are we going to do that?"

"I'd need to think about it. But I'm going to be more valuable to them in a year or two. They're going to need me as a witness. They're not going to worry about whether I ran off or not."

She didn't look at him. What had sounded firm and even reasonable when he was saying it now revealed itself as stagey, absurd.

He shook his head, walking away.

He had been worse than a fool, but he'd never thought he'd done anything wrong. There was that moment in the coffee shop when he'd finally understood that Tony Serra was not just stealing from him, but that Serra could put him in jail or even have him killed. He had not known how it had happened at first, thinking that the buyers were just defaulting—that they were people on fixed incomes, old people, people who'd got in over their heads. It had taken him a long time to realize that his own salesmen had been manufacturing worthless contracts—not only Serra but others. The banks and finance companies were calling in the debts that he had personally guaranteed—three million dollars in loans he had personally guaranteed. For months now, they'd been offering less and less for his paper. But if he wanted to keep the company alive long enough to try to fix the problem, he had no choice but to keep selling the paper.

"I'll take care of it," Warren always said. "It's my money we're talking about, too. I'll fire the pricks."

It was true, he would fire the salesmen. Cornwall would watch him do it, Warren blunt but somehow also genial even then. But it was Warren who would hire the replacements. It took Cornwall a long time to really believe that Warren held him in such utter contempt: the cracker from Eugene, the rube with the Baptist face. You trusted people. You trusted them longer than you would have imagined. It took Cornwall a long time to really believe that Warren had never cared about how the sales got made, as long as they got made, as long as Warren got paid his monthly disbursement.

There was always more land. There was always a whole state of sunlit, empty land that you bought for $30 or $40 an acre, then sold for twenty or thirty times that. There was always the hope that by selling more land you could begin to cover your losses, a conviction you held more stubbornly as it became less and less true.

He remembered the night he'd brought home the white Rolls-Royce Silver Shadow. He couldn't believe it was in the garage.

It had a phone in the backseat, and on special occasions he'd hire one of the office boys to put on driver's livery and act as his chauffeur.

———

St. Patrick's Day—the first time Lonzo McCracken ever saw Warren, standing at the bar at Navarre's restaurant a little after two o'clock in the afternoon. Warren was staring down at his memo pad, smoking, unmindful of the green tinsel and the paper shamrocks hanging from the ceiling above him. McCracken wore a hunter's tan shirt beneath his sport coat, a perfunctory striped tie. He held at his waist three small notebooks bound together by three thick rubber bands. When he introduced himself, Warren appraised him slowly, exhaling from his cigarette.

"I had the girl hold a table," he said, putting the cigarette out in the ashtray. "Why don't we sit down."

They walked over to the hostess stand and Warren stood watching the girl come over, his hands in his pockets. The lunch crowd was businessmen with their jackets off, women at separate tables who weren't these men's wives but were the same kind of women as their wives—docents at the museums, iced tea and chef salad and French onion soup. Warren smiled at one of them, pulling in his upper lip and softening his eyes. He stopped and chatted with a man in an open-neck sport shirt, Warren's hand on the man's shoulder, the hostess and McCracken not looking at each other, both knowing they were being made to wait. When they finally sat down, Warren spread his napkin on his lap and stared at the detective.

"I come here quite a bit," he said. "As you can see. Not usually with a cop."

McCracken put his three rubber-banded notebooks on the table and kept his hand on top of them. "I appreciate you meeting me."

"Well, that's fine as long as lunch is on you."

He didn't smile, but he was less abrasive after that, more soft-spoken than McCracken would have expected, East Coast, urbane. What he said had been prepared in advance but was delivered in such a casual tone that it suggested an unspoken, obvious understanding between them. He was a businessman in the community, he began, a cliché that produced something like a mild sleepiness, a difficulty in paying attention. His friends were some of the most important people in the city. He was a supporter of the Phoenix Symphony Orchestra. It didn't make him happy to be talking to a cop in a public place. It didn't make him happy to be the subject of controversy. His past had been aired in the newspapers several years ago and he didn't relish the idea of going through all that again. He had loaned James Cornwall money. He had loaned Tony Serra money. It had been a mistake in both cases, but he had loaned a lot of people money, he had set up a lot of people in business, he had made a lot of people very wealthy. What he was asking for now was a few weeks to pull some money out of Great Southwest, and then he would speak with McCracken at greater length about all he knew.

A man walked into the bar, holding a newspaper, searching the faces, then approached their table. He wore a navy suit and a pale green shirt and a plaid tie. McCracken slowly recognized him. He was the prosecutor Moise Berger's land fraud investigator, George Brooks.

"A friend of mine," Warren said, turning. "I think you know each other already."

McCracken put his menu down, but didn't stand up. He looked neutrally at Brooks, who blankly extended his hand across the table. Warren lit a cigarette and blew a fine blanket of smoke over the basket of rolls.

"We were just talking about Great Southwest," he said. "I think you both also know Jim Cornwall."

Brooks didn't respond or even seem to hear. He sat down and now he was studying Warren's menu and he didn't say a word until they ordered.

McCracken thought of Serra, of their conversation a year earlier in the Pullman Pie. *You're going to have a hard time getting anywhere with this. Warren, those people, they've got everyone tied in.*

———

I'll have my lawyer call Mo Berger, the county prosecutor. Our friend Moise Berger.

———

Ed put down the phone. Through the slats of the office blinds, the harsh light of early dusk flared white and orange, then left a violet haze when he closed his eyes. The phone call had been from one of his oldest loan sources, Gene Silver at Talcott Financial. Gene Silver had said that the top brass at Talcott were putting a stop on all land developer applications at this time because of "trepidations on a recent spate of negative publicity about the industry." Silver said that in Consolidated's case there were concerns about mortgages held by overseas buyers—soldiers over in Japan or the Philippines who had almost certainly never seen their properties. He reminded Ed that Talcott had lost several thousand dollars recently on land company paper from Arizona firms. He reminded Ed of a recent article in *Time* magazine about deceptive practices in the land business. It was nothing personal, Silver said, but there was risk aversion, and if the story had made it into *Time* magazine, then it was hardly news to anyone who followed the industry or had money in it.

Ed remembered the article from *Time* magazine. He remembered it, because it had come out the same day as his lunch at Durant's with James Kieffer and the executives of CMS.

He rubbed his eyes, then blinked them into focus. When Gene Silver had mentioned the overseas buyers, Ed lost his temper. *What are you implying? No, what are you implying?* But even as he said these things, he knew that anger never sold anyone on anything.

13

Five minutes to midnight—Barbara was asleep. Warren made himself a Scotch and walked back into the living room, his dog at his heels, the last of his two Dobermans, its long pink tongue hanging sideways over its teeth. He gave the dog a flick on the snout and bent down over it, petting its throat. There were only a few lamps burning, no music, just the banal reverie of his own thoughts, the kind of after-hours solitude that made him feel weightless, detached. In the beige light, he looked for a moment at the room: the telescope on its mount, the stone fireplace, the settee with its zebra-skin print, a touch of the hunting lodge. He sipped his drink, assessing it as a stranger might assess it. Outside, the view was black through the window glare. He cleared his throat and walked over and looked out at the city: a palm-studded valley under the dark sky, cars reduced to small pricks of moving headlights, no people visible. It all moved and moved without him—the bars and private rooms, the restaurants—all of it hidden in darkness, softened beneath the glow of the streetlights. Even the palm trees seemed placed there as a form of concealment.

The plays had been to give the loan to Brooks, the loan to

Kieffer, to pay off Talley, then to sacrifice Cornwall and maybe Serra. He'd had to appease Serra because of Serra's connections. Serra, the goombah, claiming a piece of the action. You gave it to him and no one could call you greedy, then you let him bury himself in his own bad decisions. It was just luck that Cornwall had appeared, the kind of open-faced American that Warren was always looking for. Cornwall had been managing a car dealership, had impounded a few cars from Warren's salesmen, and that's what had got them talking—"I like your spirit," that kind of thing. You read his résumé and saw he'd been to Bible College and you sensed the other tendency ready to burst into full flower. It was a hunch, an instinct, putting them together, Cornwall and Serra, like a cat and a snake in a gunnysack, the kind of intuition that came to you after forty years of living by your wits.

He walked over to the phone and looked for the number in his memo pad, turning the pages with his thumb. According to his watch, when he dialed the first digit, it was twelve midnight exactly.

"This is Ned Warren," he said, his voice quiet, curious, as if he were answering the call and not making it. He looked back down at the rotary dial of the phone as he put down the memo pad. He pictured Cornwall blinking himself awake in the now lamp-lit bedroom, his wife rolling over beneath the tangled sheets. "Why don't you pick up on the other extension," he went on. "The one in the kitchen. Go on, rise and shine. I want to discuss something with you."

He took another sip of his Scotch, facing the bookcases now. He imagined the layout of Cornwall's house. He knew the layout because he and his son-in-law, Gale Nace, had gone to look at it just days ago with the idea of Gale making an offer on it.

"What is the idea—"

"Just take it easy. Are you in the kitchen?"

"This is out of line. You have no business calling me up in the middle of the night like this."

"My son-in-law came by tonight. Gale. We were talking again about your situation with the house. I'm trying to help you, that's why I called. Gale said he wants to make you an offer. He said he would offer you sixty thousand, and I told him no, that wasn't right, the house was worth twice that, he had to come up. I think there's room to negotiate, that's why I'm calling you. I'd ask Gale for seventy. I'd take sixty-eight. I'd get it settled this week, get it over quickly. Then I'd get out of the country as soon as possible."

There was silence. Warren looked across the room at the windows. He could see a faint image of himself reflected there, a primitive figure—head, shoulders, arms. He knew that Cornwall was realizing what time it was, that timing the phone call at the stroke of midnight had not been accidental.

"I can pick up the phone and have someone maimed or killed," Warren said. "I think you should know that. I have to play ball with Serra because of who Serra works for, but as far as I know, the only person you work for is me."

Ed looked at the plats, the streets and numbered lots of Verde Lakes I, Verde Lakes II, Verde Lakes III, Chino Meadows. *A subdivision of the N.E. of the N.W. 1/4, the N. 1/2 of the N.E. 1/4, the S.E. 1/4 of the N.E. 1/4, the E. 1/2 of the S.E. 1/4 of Sec. 23, T 16 N, R. 2 W.* The words were written in pencil in a neat hand: the surveyor's notations on percolation and curve data, the compass points for the sites of drainage easements. White Cap Drive, Palo Verde Drive, Ponderosa Trail, Bottle Brush Court. Improvising, narrowing one of his eyes, Warren had laid out these street names with the dry efficiency that Ed brought to a column of numbers. It was his gift, the instinct for names that were slightly corny, evocative of real, affordable places, not just fantasies. He had come up with Lazar Road for the large diagonal thoroughfare, and then Ed had suggested the small cross street, Zachary Lane—he might not have been so whimsical without Warren's example. Tumbleweed Drive, Apache Lane. Eventually the names took on a jokey, fatigued absurdity: Jackrabbit Trail, Coyote Corner, Leaping Lizard Lane. There were streets named for wives and ex-girlfriends: Susan Street, Donna Drive, Portia Place, Yvonne Way. It became

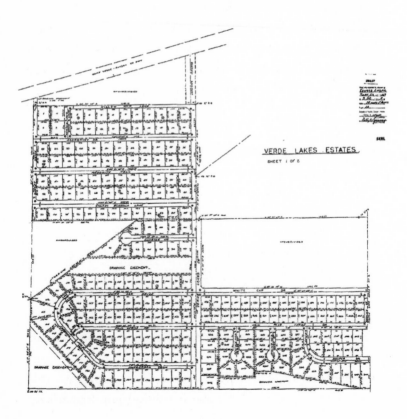

VERDE LAKES ESTATES

SHEET 1 OF 2

a kind of game. When they'd finished mapping it out, Ed took the surveyor's plans to Prescott and got the stamps and the requisite signatures: the county recorder, the health examiner, the engineer, the notary public, everything legal, everything by the book.

He had heard from another contact in Sacramento, Dale Sitka, one of the VPs over at First Financial, that American Home Industries, Consolidated's parent company, was having credit problems. According to Dale Sitka, AHI was stretched very thin. The housing business in California had started to slow down. If interest rates went up a point or two, then AHI would find itself hard-pressed to keep current with its loans. They would be facing a potential bankruptcy. Sitka said that some investors were already making bets on what the Fed would say next week, and Ed should keep a close eye on the NASDAQ.

> Dear Ed,
>   Enclosed find a copy of promissory note from James Kieffer. Consolidated Acceptance Corporation is assigning one-quarter of the proceeds of this note to Consolidated Mortgage Corporation in exchange for your remittance to Consolidated Acceptance Corporation, in the amount of $650. Period.
>   Very truly yours,
>   Consolidated Acceptance Corporation,
>   N. J. Warren

The memo was like an image of his own qualms and bad faith.

He called his lawyer, Phil Goldstein. It was not a good time to be thinking about getting out of the business, but he wanted to discuss what it might cost him to do so anyway.

"I'm glad you called," Goldstein said. "I was going to call you. When was the last time you spoke to Ned?"

"We're not on the best of terms right now."

"Well, that's fine. That's just fine. Can I tell you something?"

"What?"

"You're not going to like this. You better sit down for this."

It was Goldstein's habit to get sarcastic just when things were at their least funny.

———————

"They've closed up shop," Tony Serra told McCracken over the phone. "Cornwall's gone—disappeared."

McCracken stared down at some evidence sheets in their folder. "What do you mean 'disappeared'?"

"He left the country or something. No one knows for sure."

"When?"

"Last Friday, they filed for bankruptcy. Kieffer had his guys put everything on hand trucks. They carted it off. They went down and seized the books."

"Kieffer?"

"Jim Kieffer. Talley's office."

McCracken thought of Cornwall sitting in the coffee shop last week, his food untouched, promising that this wouldn't happen, that he wouldn't flee.

He hung up and put his jacket on. He took the elevator down to the parking lot and then he started up Central Avenue in his car, forcing himself to drive slowly, his stomach distended, chest burning.

He took a deep breath and let it float up into his head. A good, deep breath and you felt the heat dissipate, a rational distance between yourself and the moment that was about to flare out of control.

There were cars in the lot on East Camelback—everything looked completely ordinary. In the building's lobby, the directory still listed Great Southwest Land and Cattle in white letters on the black board. But Serra was right. Almost everyone but Cornwall was still there, but the books had disappeared.

———

In the offices of Consolidated Mortgage, the phones rang, they were answered, but the typewriter keys struck only sporadically, thin clicks against the platens, the transistor radio low but somehow impertinent amid the solemnity of closed doors, the men in their emergency meeting. In his office, Ed did some calculations on a yellow pad, using rough figures he knew by heart—salesmen's commissions, office overhead, roads and utilities, payroll, accounts receivable, accounts payable. He was determining the slimmest margin Consolidated could operate on, now that there would be no more money coming in from AHI, which had just frozen its credit lines. Warren's hair showed gray between the dark furrows. You looked at him and saw an investor, nothing more or less stolid than that. He watched Ed, guessing the figure in advance, and Ed put down his pencil, looking not at Warren but at Phil Goldstein, the lawyer, who leaned back with his cigarette drawn behind his head, the kind of gesture a film director might make after finishing a take. Before Goldstein were the folders, laid out on the conference table like tiles—Consolidated Mortgage, Great Southwest, Cochise College Park, Queen Creek, Prescott Valley—all of Warren's empire, company by company, in each folder the documents showing where each company got its financing. On top of each folder was a mark indicating which company's paper was still good, which was not, which paper might still be attractive to underwriters like First National Bank or ITT or Westinghouse, now that the land market was collapsing.

"We can go to about twenty-one percent," Ed said. "That's the most we can discount. After that, we're running a loss."

Warren wiped two fingers blearily down his cheek. "We won't have to go that deep," he said. "But it won't hurt to tell AHI we're going that deep."

Goldstein came out of his recumbency. He was a large, bearded man, a blond Jew who could wear suspenders and a silk bow tie because he had played football in college. "You want your stock back," he said.

"I want the stock back because it's still worth something," Warren said. "Consolidated is worth five million dollars. In a few months, AHI will be worth nothing. Why should we be helping them out?" He twisted the paper wrapper off a lollipop, frowning down as it tore and stuck to the candy.

"'We will sell paper until such time as AHI can resolve its credit issues,'" Goldstein said, as if dictating the letter already. "'We will sell this paper at substantial discount, likely running Consolidated at no profit in this interim period.'"

"Let AHI think about it for a while," said Warren.

Ed pushed the yellow pad away from him and looked back over his ledger. He would have to not panic. If they forced this split from AHI, then it would be his problem, not Warren's. It would be up to him, not Warren, to keep Consolidated running at no profit in this interim period.

He had signed a personal guarantee on the loan for the Oklahoma land. There would be no easy way to walk away from the business, even if he wanted to.

———————

McCracken drove up Central Avenue to North 44th Street and parked in the lot of the Real Estate Department, the warrant in his jacket pocket, on the opposite side from his gun. He took the elevator to the fifth floor, then walked the gray linoleum hall with his three rubber-banded notebooks in his hand.

"I'm here to see Fred Talley," he said to the girl at the desk.

There was a man standing behind her, leaned against the wall. He was James Kieffer, McCracken realized. Jacketless, in a red tie and a white short-sleeved shirt, he crossed his arms.

"If you know where Jim Cornwall is, I need to talk to him," McCracken said.

"I have no idea where Jim Cornwall is," Kieffer said. "Did you try his home?"

"I need to see the Great Southwest records. Right now. I know they're here."

"Go yell at Berger's office," Kieffer said. "They're the ones that made the call."

McCracken took the warrant out of his breast pocket. He smoothed it out slowly on the counter, running the edge of his hand over the piece of paper, then held it up.

"I'll call Berger's office right now," Kieffer said.

McCracken followed him back into the maze of desks, the gray steel file cabinets, the coffee urn on its stained plastic card table. Talley's door was ajar. He looked at McCracken and frowned, his mouth open. He was eating some kind of sandwich out of a paper bag.

"Do I need to call my lawyer?" he said.

"I don't know. You tell me."

"You wait right there until I call my lawyer."

A $5 million fraud. Not just one bankruptcy but many. Not just Cornwall's Great Southwest but the companies who financed their paper or did business with them. The land business was a confidence game. The value and sale of real estate is always something of a confidence game, but no one anticipated how quickly everyone could lose confidence. It didn't matter if you were playing it basically straight. Before long, no one was very interested in the investment potential of Arizona land.

Ed went through the papers in his desk, the memos and pamphlets and brochures. He thought of Cornwall hearing about the AHI deal last spring, seeing it as a glint of hope. *I could use the financing more than you could—you know that. If there's any way you could put in a word for me, I would appreciate it.*

How unlikely it all was. How unlikely that less than a year later they would both be in so much trouble. How unlikely that AHI would fall apart the exact same week that Great Southwest fell apart. How unforeseeable that his life would end up so resembling James Cornwall's life.

———

The rock face in sunlight. The tufts of dry grass pushing through the sand. The hiss of insects, the sudden flare of grasshoppers. The pointless shades of brown, the grass putting forth its blades.

———

When he got home, the house smelled like vinegar. They had been dyeing Easter eggs, Susie and the kids. Zachary was dressed like an Indian brave with black yarn for braids and paint on his face. Stacey was crying in her high chair. It had taken only the length of his drive home from the office for the office to seem like a phantasmagoria. In the space of a day, he had lost everything. He shook his head at Susie, then rolled his eyes, then smiled, mock-scolding her for bringing Easter eggs into their Jewish home. Zachary held one up, his mouth gaping, struggling not to drop it.

14

"He had nurtured prostitution and gambling in Phoenix for years," declared the report. Rosenzweig once owned apartments that were rented out to prostitutes whom he supplied to visiting businessmen. References to him as the "Diamond Man" were found in prostitutes' "trick books."

—*Time*, March 28, 1977

April 28, 1975—Members of the Phoenix police intelligence squad invite (Moise) Berger to a meeting in the I-squad office. They confront him with several items discovered during the investigation which they felt might affect Berger's effectiveness in the Warren prosecution: that he had been dating a secretary who worked for a Warren-connected land company; questions about his lack of prosecution on the Warren-related Arizona Land Co. fraud; a stack of Arizona Land Co. forgeries and fraud evidence that had been "lost" by Berger's office; a statement

attributed to Berger that no Jew would go to jail
as long as he was county attorney; and the bribery of Brooks—Berger's investigator—by Warren aides. Berger denies all.

—*Newsday,* **March 24, 1977**

This was Phoenix in the late 1960s and '70s, a caricature of itself.
This was the Phoenix in which my father was murdered. In
some other kind of city—if there is another kind of city—things
might have gone differently. He refused police protection when
he finally had to testify against Warren. He refused, I think,
because he couldn't believe that he lived in the kind of city where
witnesses were murdered on their way to a grand jury.

The night I arrived in Phoenix was unusually cold, even for
December, and a thick fog hung in the courtyard of my hotel, sent
up from the vast, heated swimming pool. It was a slow period for
the hotel, and it seemed abandoned that night, spectral, a care-
fully maintained resort with no other guests but me, stretching
out for acres—arcaded walkways, palm trees, fountains, lawns. My
room was too big, accentuating the fact that I was there by myself.
I ironed some clothes and drank the beers in the minibar. I went
through the newspaper clippings: hooded witnesses, judges taking bribes, hit men called "Hopalong" or "One-Eyed Jack." By the
time I went back out into the dark to get another drink at the bar,
there was the feeling that it was not 2006 but 1975, that my presence in Phoenix was somehow known. I drove the next morning
to Warren's old house and when I got lost and asked someone for

directions, the woman I spoke to was an old friend of one of War-ren's daughters. The city had become my hallucination. I found my name on a street sign in Verde Lakes. I found my father's grave. I found the stairwell in which he was murdered. When the sun came out, it struck everything at a low angle, and it stayed cool, the trees and buildings cast in shadow. I felt unreal and went for a run on the treadmill back at my hotel. There was no one else there. I went back to my room and got ready for dinner.

The Scottsdale Plaza

PART FOUR

171 known gangsters, most of whom have arrived in the past ten years, reside in Phoenix and Tucson alone. They deal in prostitution, illegal gambling and narcotics smuggling; Arizona, in fact, has become the chief corridor for narcotics entering the U.S. now that Mexico has replaced Turkey as the leading source of heroin. The mobsters have gone unmolested, says the report, because "until recently the prosecutorial system has been marked by incompetence, fuzzy or nonexistent law and brazen bribe taking."

—*Time,* March 28, 1977

15

REPORT OF INTERVIEW OF
ROBERT DOUG HARDIN

CASE: OCI86-0045

DATE OF INTERVIEW: 10 DECEMBER, 1986

LOCATION OF INTERVIEW:
> OFFICE OF THE ATTORNEY GENERAL
> 1275 W. WASHINGTON
> PHOENIX, ARIZONA

PERSONS PRESENT:

ROBERT DOUG HARDIN	RH
JUDSON ROBERTS, OCRD	JR
JOSEPH KORETSKI, SID	JK
GEORGE WEISZ, SID	GW
JACK SMITH, U.S. MARSHALL	JS

JR   10 December, 1986, at 10:04 AM. Present are
Joe Koretski, Jack Smith, George Weisz, Jud
Roberts and Robert Hardin

(Introductions in background)

JR   We'll get right to the point. Uh, the reason we
want to talk to you is that we're looking at a
murder...

—————

I thought I knew this part of the story. Then a friend I'd made in Phoenix, a historian named Dave Wagner, sent me an e-mail saying he'd come across a document that might be of interest to me. It was a 214-page transcript of an interview from 1986 with Robert Doug Hardin, one of the hit men who had killed my father.

It arrived in a brown cardboard box. I wanted to read it fast, right away, but it went on and on, jumping from anecdote to anecdote, a blur of names and boasts, scattered memories of more than ten murders Hardin had committed in Phoenix and Chicago. I read it again from the beginning, this time with a better idea of what was relevant. On the third try, I began to adjust to Hardin's language, to locate his frame of reference, to recognize the intelligence, so different from my own, that lay beneath his way of speaking. I thought his way of speaking was crucial to what the transcript had to say. I sat down and pared the 214 pages down to the following eight.

—————

He was twenty years-old when he came up from Alabama, 1964, Robert Doug Hardin—they called him Doug. He was doing house burglaries in Chicago and Doug would take the gold coins and silver dollars and diamonds and sell it to Lee DiFranco, who was with Albert Tocco, he was one of Albert Tocco's soldiers in Chicago Heights. One day Doug got in an argument with a guy named Jimmy Carver, and Carver had a habit of beating everybody up, so Doug had a little old .32, one of them little things you put in your hand, he found it in a burglary. Carver grabbed ahold of Doug and Doug shot him in the stomach. The first time he ever shot anyone. Old Lee seen it. That's when they started talking—when Doug would go in the Upstairs Restaurant or the Liberty Restaurant, there'd be Lee and he'd come sit down.

One night Lee asked him to go for a ride and they just started talking and Lee said he liked him. It just growed like that. Doug got into another run-in with the Los Hombres motorcycle gang in Indiana and the two guys he was doing burglaries with ran and hid. Doug had to go to Lee like a little kid and say could he get him, a, you know, a high powered gun that shoots a lot of times. Lee said what's the matter and Doug told him. He says come on, I'll go with you. They shot them son of a bitches plum out of Indiana. And Lee would stand there and laugh as he did things like this. Lee was a different type—Lee was from the old school of that. And Tocco was from the old school.

Lee was a vicious little bastard, only five foot two, but when he came after you he got what he wanted. Doug saw him plug a guy in a wall one time, took his shoes off, tied a few cords around his throat, then stuck him in the fucking wall, electro-

cuted him. Went over and stood by the circuit, got a pitcher of water, threw it on the guy, then flipped the switch, knocked the circuit, what did he think about that? That was the cycle of Lee's mind. He was that vicious, it's just that Lee kept it low profile. And he did things in spurts. And he walked around with twenty-five, thirty, forty thousand dollars in his pocket all the time so nobody know'd he had anything he wanted.

They went to Phoenix four or five times a year. Usually they'd go for about a week at a time. Lee's brother was there, Dominick. Dozens of guys were there. There were the Englishes, Verives, Frank Pedote, Fred Pedote, Paul Schiro, Old Man Kaiser—they were all there, there was going to be lots of work in those years. Back in Chicago Heights, they were all planning Phoenix. Dominick had a big piece of land, near Prescott, land in Black Canyon near the highway, some land in Sun City. Lots of acres, maybe fifteen hundred acres. Him and a guy named Art Sobel had the real estate office, East-West Realty. Sobel was just an instrument that Dominick needed. There was no respect there. It was a tool, but there was no respect.

This was what they talked about every morning back in Chicago Heights over breakfast, how they were going to run Phoenix. Who had the politicians, who had the cops. Whether Joe Bonanno was there. Nobody in New York would have Bonanno anymore. He was a dead man in New York. They done run him out of there, didn't want nothing to do with him, so now he lived down in Tucson. He ran a cheese factory down in Tucson, he ran heroin out of Culiacán, Mex-

ico, but he kept things quiet. The only help he'd get now was maybe out of Palm Springs, unless he had the politicians. That was Lee's theory. Unless Joe Bonanno had the politicians, Phoenix was wide open. That's what Lee DiFranco and Albert Tocco were talking about. That they could handle Joe Bonanno. That they were planning Phoenix and this was their opportunity to get it, to have a war with Joe Bonanno.

They were going to shake the bush and get the lion to jump out. That was how Dominick DiFranco put it.

Doug did ten or fifteen murders in that time with Lee. He did a hit on Chick Coralsky and Chick was a friend. Doug had got Chick the job of managing the Mantino Hotel and the Mantino Hotel was a little lockdown whorehouse Lee had. It was a motel and it had sixteen rooms and the whores in each room. This was a good business, the place made a quarter of a million dollars a year. Doug and Chick were friends and even though Chick was older, Doug had sat down with Chick like a father to a son. Doug sat him down and said Chick no matter what you do, don't steal, don't break any of the rules, don't you let any of those girls crawl across the state line. They'll bust the joint and they'll confiscate it. Doug said, Chick if you break those rules, they'll kill you for it. Chick said, I give you my word kid. I'll treat it like if it was yours. Instead, he broke every rule. Damn phone bill a hundred and five dollars, girls was calling Florida, Indiana, Kentucky. They had a girl over there fifteen years old working in a whorehouse lockdown. Even though they were paying the Sheriff, what if the G had a went down there? And that was just the way it was told to Doug. Damn if Lee DiFranco didn't come and start screaming at Doug. Doug had gave Lee his word. If anything happened, if Chick broke any rules, Doug was responsible. So Lee called and said hit that mother-fucker. He was holding Doug to what their deal was. So Doug went to Chick and asked Chick did you do this? He gave him that chance. And Chick said hey fuck it, it don't mean nothing. So Doug figured if he took that attitude, ass-hole, if this prick would do this, he was a danger. Your mind had to tell you what you learned in the past. So Doug was going to grab Chick and take him to Lee, but what happened is they caught him by accident riding a horse on a Saturday afternoon. He was riding an Appaloosa horse that he had borrowed from a doctor and they just pulled up beside him and shot him off the horse with a carbine on a Saturday after-noon. That was the end of Chick Coralsky. Doug went to his wake and they were burying him without a tie and a shirt. Doug bought him a shirt and tie and made the undertaker put it on. He liked Chick as a person. It's just that Chick was on the wrong cycle. And at one point, Lee was like a father to Doug, and Lee said, come on, we got a piece of work to do.

Lee got the whorehouse in Apache Junction, outside Phoe-nix. The guy that was running it was an old white headed guy, curly hair, ugly old boy. Big old boy and they were skim-ming. And then Jackie Dowl and Johnny O. came to town. Lee wanted to burn down their joints, wanted to muscle them out. They had a joint outside Phoenix that had waterbeds in it and Doug and Lee fired it up. They fired up Johnny O.

back in Chicago on the Indiana/Illinois border. Johnny O. had a big whorehouse—go go joint, supper club—between Dower, Indiana, and Salt Village. Doug and Lee fired it up, burned it down but then Johnny O. brought his operations to Phoenix. Albert Tocco sent them there to Phoenix, so Lee had to let it slide. Albert Tocco was Lee's partner in Chicago. What he made out there, Albert got half of. The white headed guy that ran the whorehouse for Lee ran the whorehouse for Albert Tocco. Old Man Kaiser overseen it all. The white headed guy ran the day to day but Kaiser kept an eye on it. He kept an eye on Lee. Old Man Kaiser was a meat cutter. He worked in a supermarket, he was cutting meat in the back. He lived in a little house with a fenced in yard, labrador dogs. The FBI busted in his home and confiscated the guns and locked him up and he was fighting em in the courts claiming he had em for the right of hunting and they were saying you're a convicted felon. Kaiser had a prostitution ring he set up with a lawyer. Seemed like every lawyer and businessman in that state had something to do with prostitution.

There wasn't a whorehouse within fifty miles of Phoenix that Doug and Lee didn't go out and take a look at. Lee had em all wrote down in a book, he was finding out who ran em. In other words, they were shaking them down, there were at least sixty whorehouses in Maricopa County. Some of them was hotels, some of them was buildings, some of them was lounges. There was about six guys who had women there that they took to certain hotels, maybe the clerk would call them up. These were high-class call girls for businessmen. The idea was for Lee to come in and muscle the whole operation. Lee and Albert Tocco were going to take over Phoenix and their whole focus at first was gambling and prostitution. And Dominick had the *land. Dominick had thirteen hundred acres just in Yavapai County, he and that land business were worth a million dollars. He had a bank safe in his bedroom: barrel door, you had to twist it, combination it, twist it and turn the lock and then pull it out and a barrel came out and you had to use a key to get by the gate inside it. They had ten or so of Leonardo Nearman's pictures. There was a set of these gold spoons and forks, twenty-two carat gold that a king used. Had jewels in the ends of em. Stuff like that just flew around in those circles. So there was a business in stolen goods and some of it went through Dominick DiFranco and some of it went through Old Man Kaiser and some of it went through Spilotro.*

They were gonna build a restaurant out in Phoenix, then they dropped that theory. Then Dominick was gonna go into construction real big, he had construction businesses in Chicago, Joliet, but the best way Dominick could wash a lot of money was in real estate, so he bought a lot of land, he started the office with Sobel. Then he and Sobel somehow muscled the water rights for some land in Sun City. The rights belonged to a law firm, the DiContis. DiContis had an office on Central Avenue, across from the country club. They had the water rights and Dominick just stole them, he got them down on paper, they were worth half a million dollars. He was acting just like a muscle, he just muscled in on the water rights and now he was trying to sell them back to DiContis for half a million. Doug would come in with Lee by Old Man Kaiser's house or by Dominick's house and he would eat something, he would listen to them talk, and that was how he first heard about the Canadian. The Canadian was a real estater, he was the front man for the DiContis. He brought the money over in a briefcase one day, Lee said, half a million dollars of DiContis' money. Doug didn't see it, but Lee said the Canadian came by with a briefcase and that he had got the money from DiConti's law office. They were supposed to give up the water rights then, but they didn't give them. And the reason they didn't give them was it was really Joe Bonanno's money. That was Lee's theory. Lee said DiConti was the fucking fall guy for Joe Bonanno—everyone knew DiConti was Bonanno's lawyer—and Bonanno ain't got no business over in Phoenix. Phoenix was wide open, he didn't have no right down there. Lee was going back to Chicago, Tocco's telling him we're gonna go partners out there, this is gonna happen. So Lee was telling Dominick don't worry about it. Lee DiFranco and Albert Tocco could handle Joe Bonanno. It was just that simple. This was everyone sitting in the den, Dominick sitting there in his undershirt smoking a cigarette and Lee's sitting there hounding him, telling him, beating his fingers on the table telling him what's going on and Dominick listening and thinking is it happening that way?

Dominick said maybe they should back off and give back the money, just take a percentage. Lee went through the roof. He's not giving the money back—fuck DiConti, fuck Bonanno, fuck everybody. Lee hated the real estate guys. He hated Sobel, he hated the Canadian. The minute the Canadian brought the money in that suitcase Lee wanted to kill him. By the rule, you were supposed to. That was the way they all functioned, that was the way they all operated. The real estate guy, the Canadian, was threatening, he was telling him he was gonna go to the police, and Lee wanted him killed. He wanted everybody killed. Dominick says, okay, we're gonna shake the bush and get the lion to jump out.

So that February, Old Man Kaiser called the Canadian up and set up this meeting at the country club. The Canadian was an older gentleman, very polite, just said his piece and nothing more. He was a big guy with a high-hairline, maybe in his sixties. It turned into a real voiceful conversation, lots of shouting, and Doug backed Lee off, said it's a public place, there's people around, let the guy go.

Lee killed him the next time they met. He choked him right in the back of Dominick's Cadillac. They had driven back to Phoenix just a few days before. They brought three .22 pistols with holes drilled in the barrels. They hid it all behind Dominick's house—Doug didn't even know they were in the car until they got there to Phoenix. They hit the Canadian and then they hit another guy in a garage, three days later, another real estater. He worked in the same building as DiContis, worked for the DiContis' law office. Worked for Joe Bonanno. Seemed like this guy in the garage done something to Dominick DiFranco or somebody that was affiliated with Dominick DiFranco. This was right after they hit the Canadian. They buried the Canadian out in the desert in a dry creekbed and no one ever found him. Doug never even knew his name. This other guy in the garage was all over the newspapers. His name was Ed Lazar.

———

There is no mention of Ned Warren's name in Doug Hardin's 214-page transcript. Of course, Hardin would not have been told Warren's name in any case. *Lee said, come on, we got a piece of work to do.* I don't think either of them knew who Ed Lazar was or why they were there to kill him.

16

Arizona Republic, June 6, 1974:

State Probes Realty Chief;
Bribe Claimed

Allegations that monthly cash payments were collected from at least six land development firms and turned over to J. Fred Talley, Arizona real estate commissioner, are being investigated by the state attorney general's office, an official disclosed Wednesday.

Ronald L. Crismon, chief of the attorney general's Strike Force on Organized Crime, said that the payments reportedly funneled to Talley were "part of the allegations brought to my attention and which we are investigating."

The 70-year-old Talley said he knew nothing about an investigation and denied any wrongdoing. He has been real estate commissioner for about 14 years and is an attorney and former Graham County school teacher.

Other sources revealed that the investigation stems from allegations made to Phoenix police and others that ex-convict Ned Warren, once known as Nathan Waxman and an Arizona land promoter, collected the monthly cash payments and allegedly delivered them to Talley....

The original allegations were made last Aug. 30 to Phoenix police by James Cornwall, 38, former president of Great Southwest Land and Cattle Co. of Phoenix.

Cornwall, who now lives in Virginia, is under a Maricopa County grand jury indictment in connection with the financial collapse two years ago of Great Southwest. Court records show he is charged with 66 counts of fraud. He is now reported to be pastor of a non-denominational Church in Virginia.

Warren, reached at his valley home, declined to comment or even listen to the allegations made against him by Cornwall.

"I don't want to discuss it," he told a reporter....

Cornwall asserted that the monthly payments to Warren by Great Southwest were a minimum of $100. Occasionally "heat" payments of as much as $500 in Great Southwest funds were made for "problems which required extra work on the part of Talley," Cornwall is quoted in police reports.

At least five other land development companies made similar payments to Warren allegedly for Talley, Cornwall told police.

Cornwall said he made the same allegations "about two months ago" to other authorities, including the U.S. Internal Revenue Service.

Cornwall added that he had only two con-
tacts with Talley, "both through Ned Warren."
However, Cornwall said, he had "no personal
rapport with him (Talley)."

Although he is unable to substantiate fully
Warren's alleged claim that the money collected
went to Talley, Cornwall said he is convinced it
did.

Cornwall told a reporter he doubts that Warren kept the payments "because I can't see him
(Warren) taking hundreds (of dollars). Warren
is a very egotistical guy and if, in fact, he could
pass money to Talley from other people without
it having to come out of his pocket and still be
a hero, I can see him doing it. That's why it is
believable to me."

Other payments from his company, Cornwall maintained, went to a "guy in the county
attorney's office."

"Warren told me," Cornwall continued,
"Hey, this is something—that all the land companies do. He told me 'all the companies I work
with.'"

Cornwall said that when he purchased Great
Southwest in 1970 he found that the company
had entered into certain agreements through
which the firm was obligated to pay Warren a
$500-a-week consulting fee, although Warren
did no consulting work.

At one point, as the Great Southwest financial situation worsened, Cornwall told police,
he stopped making the weekly consulting payments to Warren for "a couple of weeks."

"All of a sudden," Cornwall told the police,
"we had lots of complaints from the Real Estate

Department." So the weekly consulting payments were resumed, Cornwall added.

Cornwall told police that Warren, in effect, controlled Great Southwest while Cornwall was its president....

Meanwhile, Wednesday, Wayne Tangye, chief of the Real Estate Department's enforcement division, said his boss, Talley, attempted to intimidate him earlier in the day. Tangye said, "He claimed I was spending too much time helping the attorney general's office in real estate fraud cases."

In the end, Tangye said, Talley threatened to fire him from his post.

Arizona Republic, June 8, 1974:

Fraud Prober Demoted by Real Estate Director

Wayne Tangye, an Arizona Real Estate Department official who is helping other state authorities investigate land frauds, said he was demoted Friday by J. Fred Talley, real estate commissioner who is one of those being investigated.

Talley is the subject of a probe by the attorney general's Strike Force on Organized Crime. He has denied wrongdoing but refused to answer any questions on the matter.

Under investigation, according to Ronald L. Crismon, strike force chief, are allegations that monthly cash payments from at least six land sales firms were funnelled to Talley through Ned Warren, ex-convict land promoter.

Tangye, who has been chief of the Real Estate Department's enforcement division, said his demotion to "investigator" goes into effect Monday. The demotion notice, he said, directs him to surrender all his records to Talley. These may include records that implicate Talley, Tangye said.

Although removed from his higher post, Tangye said he will continue to cooperate with the attorney general's office, "as any good citizen would."

The Real Estate Department, Tangye said, already has a full complement of investigators.

"I was told two days ago by Talley," Tangye said, "that I was spending too much time with the attorney general's office investigating land frauds."

Tangye said he remains "vitally interested" in the investigations.

The demotion, Tangye said, means a monthly salary cut of between $300 and $350....

Arizona Republic, June 8, 1974:

Land Promoter Called Influence Buyer

A land promoter who designed and operates a vast network of fraudulent real estate schemes in Arizona has not been prosecuted because he "has purchased too much influence in this community," the court-appointed attorney for three bankrupt corporations charged Friday.

The promoter was identified as Ned Warren, an ex-convict, by the attorney, Bruce Babbitt.

Babbitt was named by the U.S. District Court to represent the trustees for Great Southwest Land and Cattle Co., Lake Montezuma Development Corp. and Educational Computer Systems.

All three firms were founded by Warren, Babbitt maintained.

Warren could not be reached for comment.

Although fraud was involved in the failure of these and other companies organized by Warren, Babbitt charged, "Warren has purchased too much influence in this community" and, therefore, has escaped prosecution.

Babbitt, a Democratic candidate for state attorney general, made the charge at a political meeting in Sun City.

"Public records are available," Babbitt continued, "that paint a vivid picture of how Warren organized the companies, milked the money out and turned them over to his associates to run them into bankruptcy and take the rap.

"The front men, including James Cornwall," Babbitt asserted, "have been indicted. But the prosecutors seem unable or unwilling to take on the real problem: Ned Warren."

Such large-scale land-fraud rackets as have blighted Arizona's national reputation for at least the past decade, Babbitt contended, suggest the involvement of "organized crime."

"Organized crime," Babbitt said, requires two ingredients: Sophisticated organizers and the cooperation of public officials."

The only way to stop the scandals, Babbitt said, is to conduct "a tough, thorough investigation and prosecution that will root out land fraud and those responsible once and for all."

Babbitt suggested the formation of an independent prosecutor's office which is free of political influence.

The pattern of land fraud has been "consistent, ongoing and publicly known," Babbitt asserted, without any serious effort made by public officials to stop it.

"The pattern began in the early 1960s," Babbitt recounted, "with the rise and fall of Western Growth Capital and related companies, including Diamond Valley and Snowflake Highlands."

Warren organized and directed Western Growth, Babbitt said, escaping any prosecution with the tacit cooperation of "powerful public personalities."

Most prominent of those associated with Warren in Western Growth, Babbitt said, was Lee Ackerman, a businessman and former Democratic national committeeman, state legislator and onetime unsuccessful candidate for governor.

"When Western Growth went bankrupt," Babbitt explained, "thousands of people lost their investments. They have never been compensated. No one went to jail."

The pattern established by Warren in Western Growth, Babbitt said, has been subsequently repeated in connection with the financial failure of other firms organized by Warren.

So far, Babbitt said, law enforcement officials

have bagged only the "front men" in fraudulent land operations, including Lake Havasu Estates Corp.

Although several of Lake Havasu Estates officers were "convicted by plea bargaining" involving the U.S. attorney's office last month, Babbitt said, "there is no evidence that the real organizers have been exposed."

Such land frauds continue to thrive in Arizona, Babbitt concluded, because "Ned Warren has purchased too much influence in this community.

"The press," Babbitt asserted, "has already reported the facts regarding the corruption of an investigator in the county attorney's office. Two years have passed and nothing has been done.

"The allegations regarding Fred Talley, state real estate commissioner, also are known," Babbitt said. "It is also a public fact that Talley's son has been employed by Ned Warren."

(Talley issued Warren a real estate license several years ago, even though Warren was a twice-convicted felon, after Warren hired Talley's son, James.)

————

He had almost fainted when McCracken appeared at his door in the summer of 1973. Before that, Cornwall had spent two years hiding in Europe, mostly in Switzerland. You could do business, buy groceries, but without the language, every conversation was a child's conversation of half a dozen words. He came back home. He started a new life as a pastor in Newport News, Virginia, head of the Peninsula Rock Church and Proclaim Center, following the path of his father and grandfather and brothers, all of whom were preachers.

He still didn't think he'd done anything wrong, so when McCracken found him, he decided to cooperate. He should have trusted Tony Serra before he trusted Lonzo McCracken.

———————

There was nothing in Ed's past that could have prepared his father, Lou, for what he had to tell him now. The world was no longer recognizable. His father wore a blue golf sweater and polyester pants and he seemed to barely listen, his hand on the recliner's armrest, head slightly bowed. Disgust, then quiet. Maybe not even disgust, just incomprehension. Then it was as if it hadn't happened. As if the money for Talley had never existed. They never talked about it again.

———————

Warren eased into the pool, grimacing in the sun's glare as he looked down at the steps beneath the water's surface. He moved gingerly in, the water rising to his waist, an aging man alone on a Wednesday afternoon, his breasts and shoulders beginning to sag. He ducked down into an awkward crouch, shivering a little, then moved forward, rowing with his arms.

His problem now was his own fatigue. Since last June, almost four months ago, not a day had gone by without his name appearing in the paper attached to the words "bribery" or "land fraud" or "organized crime." It required energy to always say "no comment," to put up a bland front that was not just a matter of pride but of physical safety. He felt himself becoming vulnerable to his own ego, his own mystique. It was as if he were vying with his son-in-law, Gale, and his son, Ned Jr., in some unannounced contest of vitality. He couldn't stop it with Charlotte—her crooked teeth, the sheen of stubble on her calves when she came out of the pool. Charlotte had a big mouth, always laughing too loud, breaking her wineglass, flirting with someone's kid in the middle of a fundraiser. There would be tears from Barbara, gossip added to the gossip. He and Charlotte would meet the next afternoon for margaritas at the Embassy Hotel. They were the actions of someone who was already starting to lose. He saw this but couldn't stop.

Tony Serra, eight to ten years in prison. Warren's old friend and partner Bill Steuer, dead of carbon monoxide in his own garage. Seven officers and employees of Great Southwest convicted, two of them sentenced to jail time, all put there by James Cornwall. Warren had known Bill Steuer since the 1940s, when they had put together their fake Broadway play, *The Happiest Days*. He and Steuer had celled together in Sing Sing. Every day there was another article about Sing Sing, about the Talley bribes, the loan to George Brooks. Every day he waited for it to balloon into a federal case.

He got a call from his lawyer, John Flynn, that afternoon, September 25. Five months of hearings and now they were coming after him for something so dubious and minor that it seemed like a ruse. He'd given a deposition last summer to the county grand jury looking into Great Southwest, then he'd given another deposition to the U.S. attorney. The two statements had inconsistencies. Moise Berger was claiming this constituted perjury. He claimed this even though he knew the statements were made in two different venues and were mutually inadmissible.

"Perjury," Warren said. "They'll get me for jaywalking next."

"It's chickenshit stuff, for the newspapers. Just go through the motions and I'll try to keep the cost down," his lawyer said.

He watched Charlotte move across the dark room through the crowd, her hair like a tattered wig, bare shoulder blades in the halter dress. The red-lit lounge insinuated an outflare of blood. Amyl nitrite, methedrine, cocaine. Chickenshit stuff, perjury, but they were coming for him. He started thinking about someone like Dominick DiFranco with thirteen hundred acres in Yavapai County. That was the way things were moving: an alliance.

———

Charlotte entwined her way around John Adamson's arm at the doorway of the Happy Garden, a swinger and lesbian bar on Indian School Road. Adamson was neuter to her, he knew, one of the big guys who could be counted on to pretend it was nothing, an older brother figure. Adamson drank a quart of vodka a day and sold stolen jewelry out of the trunk of his wife's car and occasionally he worked a shift at places like the Happy Garden, one of the places Ned Warren ran with Ned Jr. and Gale Nace. Adamson wore two-tone shoes and tinted glasses, even indoors and at night. He bowed his head and made the faintest gesture toward a sheepish grin, and Charlotte banged her open palm against the lapel of his leather coat, confident that she saw right through him, so out of it she didn't remember she'd been writing him bad checks for the past three months. The checks were his insurance against Warren—that was why he never said anything. If the bad checks ever fell into the wrong hands, then Charlotte would end up having to answer a lot of questions from Lonzo McCracken. For example, how did she get her job at the Happy Garden? Answer: Ned Warren had gotten her the job. How could Ned Warren get her a job at a bar owned by Dennis Kelly? Answer: Ned Warren was the person who actually owned all of Dennis Kelly's bars. Was it Mr. Warren who ordered the monthly payments to John Adamson's company, Parking Control Systems? Yes. And what services did John Adamson's company provide?

You firebombed a bar with dynamite, or C-2 or C-4 in an amber-colored cylinder with a valve built into the side for the twelve-volt cap. You could firebomb the Happy Garden with a few of these cylinders slotted right into the ends of Dennis Kelly's tiki torches, but Little Huey's was in a black neighborhood, so Adamson and Carl Verive used ordinary Molotov cocktails. Maybe the Panthers did it. Black neighborhood, white owner, the Kellys an old Phoenix family. They knew going in that there would be no police investigation anyway, beyond the first perfunctory report for the insurance.

Verive held the trunk door open with his extended hand, squinting down into it, then slammed it shut on the wadded, gasoline-smeared towels. He weighed two hundred and thirty-five pounds and he had slicked-back hair and a face like Johnny Cash, thick sideburns almost down to his jaw, the long points of his shirt collar hanging out over his jacket lapels. In the trunk was a length of steel cable with taped grips, covered with blood and hair. Adamson had seen it before. That was Carl Verive. It was through Carl that he had met all the other Chicago people—the Pedotes, the DiFrancos, Paul Schiro, Old Man Kaiser. You came into the darkness of the bars and there was always a glass full of red plastic cocktail straws, hushed lighting on the bottles. The Ivanhoe, the Phone Booth, the Scotch Mist, Rudy's. Adamson had watched them evolve, watched people like Carl Verive and his friends slowly take them over.

"Honey's first bar," he said, when they were back in the car.

"Who's Honey?" Verive said.

"Honey is Dennis Kelly. I told you that."

Little Huey's was barely on fire, but the windows were smashed in and there would be smoke damage. Adamson took a sip of vodka.

"Honey," said Carl Verive.

"It's what Warren calls him. You never heard that?"

Verive didn't look at him. He had settled into his seat, was waiting for Adamson to shut his door before he started the car. He stretched his arm out the opened window.

He wasn't real to Charlotte. She would blather at him in her Texas voice, always talking on her phone to someone else, and John Adamson would stand there in the back office with his hands balled together before his groin—John who worked the door, John who striped the parking lots with new white paint. She didn't know he kept meticulous records in a formal day planner, so that along with the bad checks he had the dates, amounts, and check numbers all written down in case he ever needed them in court. She didn't know he would be famous some day. They would call him John Harvey Adamson then. They would have to use all three of his names once he had committed his first murder.

Dennis Kelly came walking into Durant's one afternoon in a white mesh shirt and faded jeans. He actually screamed when he saw Carl Verive sitting at the bar. Kelly was screaming, *Don't kill me! Don't kill me!* and everyone in the restaurant heard and Adamson had to walk over and calm him down. He was tired of Honey by then, but the last thing he wanted was a public scene.

They went to the New Town Saloon to talk. They got a booth and Adamson ordered a vodka and he told Kelly to stop fooling around, to pay Warren the $100,000 he owed. He didn't like chasing Dennis all over town, he had had enough of it. He wasn't even getting paid for it anymore, as Kelly knew from his own bankbook, where all those bad checks had come from.

"You should never have talked to McCracken," Adamson said, leaning forward. "He can't help you anyway. No one's afraid of McCracken. They've got him boxed in on every side."

Kelly's white mesh shirt seemed to glow against his tan skin. He looked away. They called him "Honey" because he was gay. He was broad-shouldered and heavy-jowled, with the black hair and bushy eyebrows of a car salesman. He ran six or seven bars, and now they all belonged to Warren and Ned Jr. and Gale Nace.

"Just keep me away from Carl Verive," he said. He reached into his pants pocket and put a roll of bills on the table in front of him. It looked like about two hundred dollars. "I get the point," he said, then left.

Adamson remembered the bad checks from Charlotte and Kelly. He called Warren at his Camelback Mortgage office, but Warren wasn't there or he wasn't taking Adamson's calls.

The next day, he was subpoenaed to a federal grand jury. The agent identified himself as Clint Brown, FBI, Chicago. He said that Dennis Kelly was in the federal witness protection program.

He said that Dennis Kelly had told him that Adamson and Ned Warren were threatening his life.

———————

A federal case. Not just McCracken anymore, but the FBI. Not just perjury, but extortion, maybe worse. That's what Adamson had told Warren. The investigators would have facts and rumors now from every Mafia source from California to New Jersey. Every Mafia source from California to New Jersey would know about the probe.

One hundred seventy-one known gangsters in Phoenix, arriving over the past ten years, a kind of invasion. Warren had watched Ned Jr. start to emulate their style. Ned Jr. had come back from Vietnam and then spent fifteen days in Pima County Jail for assault, acting just like a muscle. Gale got hooked on the idea of himself as Sonny Corleone. It had never been Warren's style. He had always told people that he lived by his wits, not by "fists or hard-guy attitude." He set Junior and Gale up with some bars. He tried to help them out. He bought Junior the Broken Arrow, on North 7th Street, and the bar became a money loser, a place Junior used mainly as a place to sleep with the help. Eventually they sold it off to Dennis Kelly and made Kelly a partner. Kelly took out a loan then to turn the old Roman Gate Cocktail Lounge into the Happy Garden, and as a favor Warren assigned the loan to Gale. That's when the threats began. It took about three months before Kelly realized that he owed Warren and Gale everything he had, and that Gale was determined to break his legs.

Warren ordered a French dip and a Dry Sack to sip on while he waited. It was October 2, a week after his first indictment from the county, the feds now involved, a vulnerable time. The restaurant was dimly lit and the table's thick, coffee-colored wood had a deep grain that felt good beneath his hand. Applegate's Olde English Pub was another place the mobsters liked. Adamson showed up when Warren was half finished with his lunch. He was followed by Carl Verive, whose mustard-colored jacket bulged open to reveal the girth of his trunk. The room, with its brass and dark carpets, became vivid, slow-moving. Verive took a seat at the wood-paneled bar and Warren picked up his sandwich end and dunked it in the au jus sauce. Adamson sat down on the banquette across from him, his big head seeming to teeter on his neck as he hunched in—sunglasses, open-neck shirt, a turquoise bracelet around his wrist.

"I'd like to have those checks before we get into this," Warren said. "The ones Charlotte wrote." He wiped his mouth and sat back. "I'm going to make sure Dennis pays you for those. I don't know if Charlotte did it, or maybe Dennis told her to do it, but it never should have happened."

Adamson placed his hands sideways in a steeple on the table, studying them as though to see if they were clean. It seemed to Warren that he was trying to remain deliberately motionless. He made a very slight shrug toward the bar, where Verive sat with his arm extended on the counter, fingering an ashtray.

"I brought Carl along when I went to see Dennis the other day," he said. "He just sat at the bar like he's sitting now. I didn't have to make any threats, in other words. Carl was sitting there. I don't know what Honey told the feds, but I never even had to raise my voice with him."

Warren looked at him, lighting a cigarette. "You're upset about not getting paid," he said.

"Not upset."

"I apologize for it, it was stupid. You're doing me a favor by giving me the checks back. When you go to the grand jury, why don't you take Mickey Clifton with you? He's a good lawyer and I'll pay for it."

Adamson unclasped his hands and tapped the table. "I told Dennis it was time to pay what he owed. I was firm with him, but I never touched him and I never had to make a threat, because I brought Carl with me. Just the sight of Carl is usually enough to get the message across, do you know what I mean?"

Warren pushed aside his plate. He let out a long stream of smoke, one eye squinted slightly, the other watching Adamson, a show of alert wariness backed by self-assurance. "What if I told you I want to have three people killed?" he said. "Could you get me a price for that?"

"What?"

"Don't say 'what.' Is that something you can do, or did you and Carl just come in here and try to strong-arm me?"

"I'm not stupid enough to try to do that."

"Given what you've been telling me about this grand jury you're going to. Given my problems in the courts. Given this little story you keep telling me about taking Carl to go see Dennis. I'm asking you if you can look into what I just asked you, or do you want to just give me the checks and I'll pay you the money and that will be it? We'll all just go our separate ways. Or maybe I should go talk to Carl myself."

Adamson didn't answer. Warren took another drag of his

cigarette, then crushed it out in the ashtray. Then he stood up and walked away from the table. He knew that Verive could sense from his spot at the bar that the stakes had just been raised. He looked right at him until Verive finally looked back. Then he went into the bathroom and waited for Verive to join him there.

From a summary of an interview of John Harvey Adamson conducted by Phoenix Police Detective Ed Reynolds, May 3, 1995:

...Adamson then went over again about how Ned Warren asked him how much it would cost to murder or could he arrange to have three murders done. Adamson explained to me that Talley at the time was the current real estate commissioner. Adamson stated that at the time he assumed that Talley was also going before the grand jury. Adamson had never heard of Ed Lazar. Ned Warren did not say why he wanted Lazar killed. Again Adamson emphasized the fact that he does not remember who the third person was. He also did not remember why this third person was to be killed....

At this point in Adamson and Ned Warren's conversation, Ned Warren got up and said he had to go to the bathroom. Adamson watched Ned Warren as he got up and walked by Carl Verive who was sitting at the bar. Adamson could see that Ned Warren said something to Verive as he walked by. A moment later Carl Verive followed Ned

Warren into the bathroom. About fifteen minutes later Adamson stated that he walked into the bathroom to see what was going on, when he could hear that Ned Warren and Carl Verive were talking about Lazar. Adamson then turned around and walked out of the bathroom alone. Later Adamson would leave the bar with Carl Verive. He stated that they did not discuss what Carl and Ned talked about in the bathroom. I asked Adamson why? And he replied that you just don't do that....

I asked Adamson if Lee DiFranco was in town at the time this was going on. Adamson advised me that he didn't know. I asked him if Lee DiFranco associated with Carl Verive? He stated that he knew that the two knew each other. He had seen Lee DiFranco and Carl Verive together around 1974 at Rudy Baragan's bar which was called "Rudy's." This bar was located on East Camelback Road. Carl Verive dropped out of sight around 1974 to 1975 when he possibly went to California. I asked Adamson if he had ever heard that Carl Verive was involved in the Ed Lazar murder? Adamson advised me that he had only heard rumors about this, but had no firsthand knowledge of Carl ever being involved.

From a summary of an interview of John Harvey Adamson conducted by Lonzo McCracken, August 8, 1979:

ADAMSON said that after LAZAR was killed he had a conversation with CARL VERIVE at VERIVE'S home located on the west side of Phoenix. VERIVE told ADAMSON that NED WARREN SR. had talked to VERIVE in the restaurant in Applegate's and had asked VERIVE to kill LAZAR. VERIVE said that he went to PEDOTE to get it done. ADAMSON said that VERIVE was acting like it was a very big deal. A little later ADAM-SON said he went to Papa Joe Tocco's place to see ROSSI. When he went in PEDOTE was sitting there in a chair. PEDOTE asked ADAMSON if he had heard anything about…WARREN using queer money (counterfeit money). ADAMSON said that he had not heard of anything like that and did not know the WARRENS fooled with that kind of stuff. PEDOTE said the payoff for killing LAZAR was to be in Los Angeles, California and "X" was to make the payoff. ADAMSON asked PEDOTE if they paid him in queer money what would he do. PEDOTE said do a couple more and not get paid for it.

17

She was a secretary at Consolidated for a little more than a year—late 1972 to early 1974—and it was sometime during then that Mr. Lazar left the firm. She remembered an office party where he gave a good-bye speech—it couldn't have been a Christmas party, but she remembered it that way. Mr. McCollum had already bought the business by then, but Mr. Lazar was still executive vice president.

She knew the company was in financial distress—everyone knew it. They worried about payroll every week, wondering if they would get their checks, and it seemed to get worse once they started the Oklahoma operation. They were selling packages because they couldn't get financing from the banks anymore. Still, everything seemed aboveboard. Mr. Lazar assigned one of the girls exclusively to call the lot buyers to go over their contracts and make sure they had signed their HUD reports. HUD was their biggest problem. She remembered calling Mr. Talley a few times at the Real Estate Department, but all the stress and worry came from HUD. They were trying to shut down every land company in Arizona, people around the office were saying.

Mr. Warren came in only once or twice a week. He was always charming, cream and sugar in his coffee.

She had never heard of Educational Computer Systems, but she thought maybe Harry Rosenzweig, who had something to do with it, had bought some packages once, though she never saw him. She never heard anything about Congressman Steiger or Senator Goldwater.

She remembered the name David Rich because Mr. Rich was going to buy Consolidated—she thought maybe he did buy it at one point. He had an English accent. Eventually, Mr. McCollum bought the company and he found a lot of debts, real problems. Lots of workers, contractors, started coming in demanding payment, very upset.

Mr. Lazar was always quiet, serious, busy. He played tennis on Wednesday afternoons, and every morning he had coffee and yogurt at the same time, 9:15. He was so concerned that she wasn't washing his spoon afterward that she bought him plastic ones. She would give him a different-colored spoon every day in his yogurt, and after that he never asked her about it again. He was very meticulous about things like that, also about his clothes and his teeth. She made his dental appointments for him. He had a beautiful smile.

———

After Consolidated ran into trouble with AHI, in the spring or summer of 1972, Warren and Ed Lazar started coming to David Rich for money. He had been a land banker going all the way back to 1959, with Lee Ackerman, just after he came over from London, but he had never owned a land company and never wanted to. Then sometime in January or February 1973, Warren came into his office and announced, "I have an offer you can't refuse." He offered all of Consolidated's stock for $100,000, with only $5,000 down. With $5,000 down, Rich would get two-thirds of the stock right away. According to the offer sheet, Consolidated had the potential to generate $20 million a year in sales. Rich knew how the finances of land companies worked, so he thought it would be closer to $1 million a year. Still, $1 million a year in actual revenue on a $5,000 down payment.

Ed Lazar was very keen on the idea. Ed came into the office and practically begged him to buy the stock. "We can run this thing," he said. Ed was an accountant, he knew the numbers—he could run the operation himself. He had brought his own father and some other relatives in as investors and he wanted to make sure they got back their money. Maybe $1 million a year for a $5,000 down payment. Rich lived to regret it, but he made the deal. After that, Ed kept coming to him for loans.

He loaned Consolidated $100,000. Then Ed came back for $250,000 more. Rich said no at that point, no more. Then in February, HUD ordered Consolidated to shut down its operations in Chino Valley. After HUD got involved, you couldn't sell land in Arizona. They made it impossible. Rich thought maybe that was when some bad sales may have been made, in Oklahoma, but that was just a guess.

Eventually he sold his shares to A. A. McCollum and Bill Nathan of Crocker Investments. His attorney would not allow him to comment on that, as there was still litigation pending.

———————

That summer was Ed's fortieth birthday, July 18, 1974. Susie threw him a big party with a Mexican theme—crepe paper decorations, a piñata. Money was still scarce, so she served miniature tacos and tostadas, and as jewelry she wore a necklace Zachary had made out of painted macaroni on a string. Their next-door neighbor Carol Nichols would never forget the party. Carol was an artist and had painted murals in Susie's daughter Stacey's bedroom. She always admired Susie's talent for entertaining, and also the graciousness of Susie's mother-in-law, Belle. At the end of the party, everyone gave Ed his birthday presents. There were dozens of packages of every shape and size, all of them beautifully wrapped, and as Ed opened them up one by one, he found that they all contained the same thing—tennis balls. More tennis balls then even Ed Lazar could go through in a year.

He looked at Susie with that smile—he had that cat-that-ate-the-canary smile. Carol had been their next-door neighbor since they moved in, and whenever her father came to visit, he and Ed would get together and try to stump each other with sports questions. Her father could be a tough nut to crack, a wholesaler in the fruit business, but Ed could always make him laugh—he was funny, smart, iconoclastic. Carol had never known Jewish men who drank, as Ed did, though she was Jewish herself. They liked to kid each other, Ed and Carol. His new office was in the same building as the Playboy Club, and one day Carol called him up, pretending to be a playmate. She put on a Southern accent and said she had heard he worked in the building, maybe they could carpool together, save on gas. He got very interested until he finally realized it was her, and he said what he always said: "You're trouble."

———

He worked as a tax specialist at LKH&H—consultant work, no clients of his own. If you looked up Ed Lazar in the phone book, you would find his home number but not his work number. When he'd left Gallant, Farrow five years before, he was bored with accounting, but now he was glad to be back doing it. For close to two years, he'd been on the verge of losing everything. Susie had had to go back to work. He'd had to check into the Homestead Act to see if their house was protected in the case of bankruptcy. It was, but every month was a struggle to make the mortgage on the $20,000 ranch house they still lived in. He was afraid Susie would leave him. He couldn't understand why she didn't. He told her to stop buying new clothes—no new clothes except for the kids. They stopped going out to eat. One morning she was doing laundry and she heard a loud pop and then a shuddering noise. The washing machine was broken—one of the plastic fins on the agitator had snapped off and the machine was full of clothes and soapy water. There was still more laundry to do. They had two young children who were always making dirty clothes. It was the one time she almost broke down in tears.

———

No clients of his own—no public role. Part of the reason was that he was facing, along with Warren and David Rich, a $1.62-million lawsuit filed by A. A. McCollum and Bill Nathan, the new owners of Consolidated Mortgage. He had almost lost his CPA license. Five years at Consolidated and the stigma would never go away. It was supposed to take eighteen months to make $1 million in the land business. After five years, he had passed the endless problem onto someone else.

———

She had grown up believing that if she married a Jewish man and knew how to bake a brisket, then everything would be all right. It wasn't true, of course, but she found this out sooner than many people she grew up with. That summer of 1974 was the happiest they'd ever been. They knew they were never going to be rich. They understood that now, but they were glad that they weren't poor.

———

He was always a sharp dresser, but one time he came over to Carol's house in a white guayabera and he kept asking if she liked his shirt. He had that smile, as if he knew how ridiculous it was, but he was playing it deadpan, and she didn't know if he was joking or if he wasn't. He was very funny. When Ronnie Fineberg graduated from law school, Ed gave Ronnie *Quotations from Chairman Bill,* by William F. Buckley. Ronnie was a liberal—Ed said it was something to fire him up before he went into court.

———

Warren said, "McCollum wanted something for nothing, and I gave him nothing for something." They almost came to blows. McCollum would say later that he got fucked to death on that deal. He spent $250,000 of his own money to buy Consolidated and it ended up costing him everything. Two accounting firms looked over the books and gave him the okay. Then he found out it was under a federal probe, that it had half a million dollars in undisclosed debts. He ended up on trial in federal court for fraud. His name dragged through the mud for nothing at all. Eight weeks later plus legal expenses, he was acquitted. Even then, he would go to the ASU football games and people who had been his friends would pretend he wasn't there.

They joined the Toastmasters Club, Ed and Ron Fineberg, but they eventually stopped going to the meetings and just went out for drinks. Newton's on Van Buren every Tuesday night. One night Ron got a call that Ed had been picked up on a DUI. He went down to find him, but there was no Ed Lazar on the blotter. He had given a different name. He said he was Eduardo Español Fuck You.

18

In early November 1974, Adamson got a call from a friend of his named Mark Rossi,* who rented a liquor store from Carl Verive's friend Old Man Kaiser. Mark Rossi knew everybody. The liquor store was near Papa Joe Tocco's bar, the Barrel, on East Washington Street, and Joe and Albert Tocco headed the Phoenix branch of the Chicago Outfit. Rossi said he'd heard from another one of the Outfit guys, Freddy Pedote, yesterday. He said that Freddy Pedote wanted Adamson to give him a call.

They were putting him in the loop, Adamson realized, which is what he'd wanted ever since he met Verive, but he saw now that there was more to it. He saw that he had no choice now but to go as far as they told him to go. They were putting him in the loop because of what he'd heard at Applegate's.

"Come over and we'll talk," Pedote said when Adamson called. "The Sun King Apartments, over on Thomas. Fifty-nine hundred East Thomas."

---

*Rossi's name has been changed.

.   .   .

The Outfit guys usually lived in run-down little houses, or they took a room at the Arizona Manor, but Fred Pedote was living in Scottsdale in one of those beige-stucco apartment complexes with Spanish tile on the roofs, a swimming pool surrounded by umbrella tables. Adamson parked in the lot with its aluminum overhang to screen out the sun. He walked into the courtyard planted with orange trees and bougainvillea, following a trail of gray concrete disks toward Pedote's door. Pedote answered in a red golf shirt, a stout man in his midfifties, the hallway behind him a dark nebulous space from where Adamson stood in the sun. He could see that Pedote was short but big, muscle under the fat. He had brown, greased hair and a mottled complexion and strange, milky blue eyes. He smelled like Old Spice. They went inside and sat down in the dark living room and Adamson had a vodka cranberry and Pedote had a Löwenbräu beer.

"Mark Rossi said you could help me get a setup," Pedote said.

Adamson stared down at the carpet, adjusting his sunglasses. "I'm not sure I know what that means."

"Mark said you knew how to make a silencer for a twenty-two pistol. We call that a setup. Okay?"

"I don't know why Mark told you that. I don't have that on hand."

"I was told you could get me one."

"I could probably make you one. I've seen it done with a plastic bottle, that's one way. But you'd be better off with a forty-five, not a twenty-two."

"I want the peashooter."

"Why?"

"That's the way we do it. It's quiet."

"I'll look into it."

"You do that."

"I said I would."

Pedote clicked on the television with the remote. He leaned back on the sofa, his legs spread apart. "Mark Rossi says you breed greyhounds," he said.

"I have a few dogs. No pups right now."

"I like the track once in a while."

"It's one of my sidelines. Just keep my hand in."

They watched TV for a few minutes without talking. It was the afternoon and the only things on were soap operas and game shows and Pedote settled on a game show. Eventually Adamson realized that Pedote was waiting for him to leave.

A few days later, he and his wife, Mary, were over at the Rossis' trailer in a suburb called Chandler. They were having drinks with Mark and his wife, when Mark said he wanted to show Adamson something out in the yard.

"They don't want the gun," he said. "They want to bomb the car. They want to make it big, send a message."

Adamson moved his feet in the gravel. There was a row of blue agave cactuses, their spines torn off at the ends like broken swords. "That's fine," he said.

Rossi nodded. He was tall and wide, like a strong man from an old circus, with a workman's battered hands. "You want to do it now?"

Adamson shrugged. "Fine. Sure."

"I've got some things in the camper. Some dynamite."

"How much dynamite do you have?"

"I've got six sticks of dynamite. I've got primer cord. Caps."

"You have magnets?"

"No."

"We'll need to go get magnets."

They told the girls they were doing an errand. Adamson stood on the porch, his back turned, while Rossi spoke through the bare aluminum screen door. They drove over to the GEMCO on McClintock and Baseline and bought some magnets and some tape. When they got back to Rossi's, Adamson just waited for him in the driveway, pretending to look over Mary's car, seeing that the tires all had pressure. Mark came back out, breathing heavily with a canvas duffel bag, frowning, and they went into Mark's camper. It was dark and hot inside, all metal and oil and dust. Mark unzipped the bag and Adamson pulled out the sticks of dynamite and set them out on the top of a strongbox. He laced them together with the primer cord, working it around and around, until he could draw the six sticks together into a loose cylinder. It was not easy and he made sure he used plenty of cord. He was just taping the ends together when Mary opened up the door of the camper and asked him what they were doing.

"Mary, go back in the trailer," he said.

She wore glasses with wide brown frames and a flannel shirt. "I see you two are up to no good."

"Go back in the trailer, all right?"

"We were going to order some pizzas. Unless you or Mark wants to go pick up a bucket of chicken."

"Pizza sounds fine. Get one. One's plenty."

"What do you want on your pizza, Mark?"

Mark was staring down into the flat of his upturned hand.

They put the bomb in a briefcase and he and Rossi drove up to the Sun King Apartments in Mary's car. The briefcase had belonged to Mary's father, a family heirloom, a brown leather contraption that opened from the top. Adamson waited in the car beneath the metal overhang while Rossi went in to make sure that Pedote was alone. Rossi's solid figure came back down the pathway of concrete disks, out of the tropical foliage, and he gave Adamson a curt, irritated wave.

Pedote was in the kitchen in a powder blue shirt over a sleeveless undershirt. He stood with his hands locked in front of his waist. On the counter was a large, iced vodka and orange juice. There was a skillet on the stove with the last shreds of some scrambled eggs stuck to its surface.

"That was quick service," Pedote said. "You want to show me how the thing works?"

Adamson let his head fall a little to one side, affronted by the tone. He was going to assert himself—tinted glasses, silver-and-turquoise jewelry—and Freddy Pedote was going to have to take it or leave it.

"Let's go outside," he said. "I'll show you how the thing works."

There were too many people around the Sun King parking lot, so Adamson said they should go over to his house across town on Minnezona. It was a one-story brick house with asphalt shingles on the roof and small square windows that had aged into a dim green. You could hardly notice the house amid the clutter of outbuildings—a toolshed, two chain-link pens for the dogs, a rusting camper shell. Around it all ran a dead lawn where Adamson parked the car beside his van. He opened up the car's hood and showed Pedote where the coil was. He was surprised that Pedote didn't know this. Mark Rossi had a light meter in his pocket and they ran a wire from the ignition coil to the light meter and Adamson turned the key from the driver's seat, the door open, and he watched Pedote watch the light meter register the charge.

"Boom," said Adamson.

Pedote stood looking at the meter in his hand, a meaningless gadget with a plastic needle that moved.

"Forget it," Adamson said. He got out of the car, more annoyed than ever now, and walked over to the house. There was an old mop bucket on the porch and he dumped the water and refilled it with clean water from the hose. Then he went inside the house and got one of the blasting caps from his closet.

"I'm going to show you what we're talking about," he said to Pedote. "You watch."

He put the cap on the wire that was still attached to the coil of the car. Then he dropped the cap into the bucket of water. He got back in the car and turned the key.

There was a sound you could hear for blocks, a dull boom flared at the edges with the fling and plash of water. The bucket lay on its side, its bottom blown out, the whole thing a different shape now. Pedote turned to Adamson, his eyes a pale, unnatural blue. He hadn't expected the power of it.

"There's people across the street," he said.

"You're right," Adamson said.

"So what the fuck are you doing?"

Adamson just stared at him. It was a stupid thing to have done. But that wasn't what had caused Pedote to look so enraged.

You couldn't see the explosion without imagining the car. The hood torn off, the windshield shattered, the doors puckered and bent. The body inside, twisted and burnt black.

A few weeks later, Adamson got a call from Pedote asking him to come back out to the Sun King Apartments. Pedote stood in the kitchen and told him they had changed plans, they weren't going to use the bomb after all, they were going to do it a different way. He wanted Adamson to take it away. He had been storing it in his refrigerator, still in the leather briefcase that had belonged to Mary's father, and the leather was cold in Adamson's hand as he walked it back out to Mary's car.

———————

Warren's perjury indictment was thrown out on October 29, 1974. The grounds were that state and federal testimonies were mutually inadmissible. Two days before Christmas, he was finally indicted for bribery—not of Talley, as everyone expected, but of George Brooks. On November 3, Talley had died of a heart attack.

19

Phoenix Gazette, July 30, 1976

Former Investigator Is Convinced
Talley Death Was Murder

James Kieffer, former chief investigator and deputy Arizona real estate commissioner, said today he believes that Commissioner J. Fred Talley was "murdered" in his St. Joseph's Hospital bed because he knew the identity of Arizona's big land fraud operators.

Kieffer thinks Talley was silenced forever to keep him from "fingering the big men" behind the state's land scandals.

"He had talked it over with his wife and he told me he would tell me the next day but he was dead by then."

Talley, 70, the record indicates, died Nov. 3, 1974, of a heart ailment, 11 days [*sic*] after being admitted Oct. 21, 1974.

Kieffer recalled that Talley was in a regular room when he called Marge Bedford, the commissioner's secretary, to ask to visit. Kieffer, at that time, was sales regulation director of the Queen Creek Land & Cattle Co., having left Talley in February 1974.

Bedford told him, the former investigator says, that Talley was out of intensive care but that he'd have to clear a visit with Mrs. Talley. He considered Talley, under whom he served, "a good friend."

The next day, Kieffer says, he called for Mrs. Talley, at her husband's side at the hospital, "but somehow I got him."

To his surprise, "Talley answered and said he would see me the next morning (Sunday) and give me the names," Kieffer declared. "Next day, he was dead.

"I think he was murdered but I can't prove it.

"It was too convenient to have died from a heart ailment when he was doing so much better. Out of the intensive care unit."

Kieffer said he reported on his beliefs at the time to a Phoenix police detective. But the detective told him that, after all, the body already was embalmed and that there was nothing that could be done to determine if Talley was murdered. Police sources claim they are unaware of Kieffer's report but say that Talley's body was autopsied. Death certificate details are secret under Arizona law.

J. Fred Talley

Ed took a photograph out of his wallet and put it down on the table to show McCracken. They were in Durant's, facing the bar with its leather bolster. There were tables of men with documents and legal pads amid glasses of ice water and cocktails, the restaurant red-lit, dim with smoke, crowded even at four o'clock in the afternoon. The photograph showed Ed's son Zachary gripping a red plastic baseball bat, many times thicker than an ordinary bat, more like a club. You could see the yellowing grass of the backyard, still glistening from the sprinkler head, the anonymous shambles on any Phoenix cul-de-sac in midsummer. Zachary wore a swimsuit and his hair was wet and he didn't know how to hold the bat, the large size of which was meant to make it easier to hit the ball. He was smiling about the game instead of concentrating on it. Ed let the photograph sit there on the table for a moment after answering McCracken's questions: the boy's name, his age. That wasn't why he'd brought it out.

"We live in a tract house, there's not much yard," he said. "You can't see it in the picture—it would be hard to take a picture with the house in it, because the backyard is so small. I never made any money in the land business like Jim Cornwall did."

McCracken looked at him with a mild but wakening scorn. He had fair, thinning hair and a slightly doughy face, not what Ed expected a detective to look like. He had the face of a school principal.

"Your son looks like a nice kid," McCracken said.

"He is. Do you have a son?"

"That's not what you want to talk to me about, is it?"

"Not right now, no. You're right."

"You want to talk to me about how different you are from Jim Cornwall."

Ed took the photograph back, holding it by the edges. "I don't have anything to say about Jim Cornwall. What I can do is back up what he says about Warren and Talley."

He'd had a meeting with Al Sitter, a reporter for the *Republic,* so he had a pretty good idea of what the grand jury was looking into— the Talley bribes, the loan to George Brooks, but not the Kieffer loan. He told McCracken that it concerned him that Al Sitter somehow always knew the details of the grand jury's "secret" proceedings and then reported on them in every morning's newspaper. It concerned him as someone who might want to cooperate now that Talley was dead. He didn't want his name in the papers, but even more important, he didn't want his father's name in the papers. The money he had given to Talley had been pissant stuff. Over four years, he had paid Talley less than $7,000. His share of the James Kieffer loan was a grand total of $650. There was a lot he could tell McCracken about Warren, but that was the extent of his own role in what the papers kept calling "land fraud" and "organized crime."

"You never actually saw Warren give the money to Talley?" McCracken said.

"No. He asked me to go once and I said no. But what I can show you is a ledger with the monthly payments. The check stubs. I can explain how the money for Kieffer was handled like the money for Talley. I have a memo from Warren telling me to pay Kieffer."

"What about Rosenzweig?"

"Who?"

"Did you ever meet Harry Rosenzweig?"

"I don't know anything about Harry Rosenzweig."

"Other public officials. Goldwater."

"I think I'm going to stop talking until I have my lawyer with me."

Warren's voice on the phone was lighter than he remembered, mellow, a little hoarse at the edges. It was the same. He hadn't heard it in more than a year.

"I've been looking into bail bondsmen," Warren said. "I thought I'd pass on my recommendations."

Ed looked at the sand-colored wall of his new office, the mild green filing cabinets, his face gradually stiffening into a meditative squint as he worked out the rationale for this call.

"I guess you know I spoke to the police," Ed said. "I wonder if you also know that I didn't reach a deal."

"You should be careful what you say to those people. For your own sake."

"They'll eventually subpoena me, they think. About Talley. I've already talked to my lawyer about it."

"Who's your lawyer?"

202 | ZACHARY LAZAR

"He said I would risk incriminating myself if I testified, so I'd have to take the Fifth. I assume that's why you're calling. You should know better than to call me here."

"This is all too bad." Warren sighed. "It really is. We'll get through it, though. You'll get through it and I'll get through it."

"I'll take the Fifth. You don't have to worry about it. Don't call me here anymore, all right?"

It should have been easier to hang up the phone. It was humiliating: the inflections of Warren's voice still acted physically on him, like a scent from childhood. He remembered their first meeting beside Warren's swimming pool seven years ago, Barbara with the silver platter of shrimp, the houses overhanging the mountainside, the Scotch sweating in his hand. *I don't know how you can stand doing taxes every year for some of the people you must have to work for. You don't seem like the type.*

He got a call later from his lawyer, Phil O'Connor. This time it was good news. O'Connor said he had just spoken with Berger's assistant, Larry Cantor, who told him they had a deal. They were going to give him immunity in exchange for his testimony before the grand jury.

————

He told the story in the broadest possible terms, and it didn't sound as serious as it was. The language of taking the Fifth, of getting subpoenaed to a grand jury, of transactional immunity, was not language he could speak to most of the people in his life, so he didn't speak it. Apart from the fear—and the fear was more easily forgotten than he would have guessed—the story *ſ*

didn't sound real even to himself. He had done nothing wrong. He wasn't worried. He didn't think he had much to tell them that they didn't already know. Even the word *immunity* was too strong, so he didn't use it either. He simply downplayed his role, saying that he couldn't believe some of the names they were asking him about in preparation for the grand jury.

Ideas make the world seem safer than it is. He was in serious trouble, but by all accounts he was never afraid.

———————

I have a transcript of his grand jury testimony. It was hard to find—I found it eventually in the Western Historical Manuscripts Collection at the University of Missouri, where there is a collection on Arizona during this time, with two whole files devoted to my father and dozens more devoted to Warren. Like so much else in this story, the history of the transcript is complicated. Being secret, technically it should never have been made public at all. It was made public in a motion filed by James Cornwall's attorney, Richard Remender, in August of 1975, after Moise Berger revoked his plea agreement with Cornwall. Remender attached the transcript of my father's testimony to show that Cornwall was not lying about the Talley bribes, as Berger claimed when he threw out the case against Warren and allowed Cornwall to go to prison for three years. Cornwall, testifying from memory, had gotten a few dates wrong on the checks he'd written to Warren for paying off Talley. Berger abandoned Cornwall over this technicality. Eventually, Warren was convicted of the bribes anyway, though not until Moise Berger had had to leave Arizona in disgrace, James Cornwall had been sent to prison, and two other witnesses—Tony Serra and Ed Lazar—had been murdered.

Hours spent in rooms—the male shabbiness of McCracken's corner of the detectives' floor, the sterile red spines of the law books on Phil O'Connor's shelves. You entered the courthouse and walked down a dreary linoleum hallway to a far corner of the building where on the gray wall was a brass sign that said GRAND JURY with a long black arrow beneath the words.

"You'll do fine," said O'Connor, who would have to leave Ed at the door. They both stood rather than sat in the waiting room with its folding chairs, wrinkled newspapers and candy wrappers littering the card tables.

Ed walked in the door and found a room like a miniature classroom, ten people seated around a fiberboard table, staring at him. They had soft drinks in wax cups, some object like a key chain or a toothpick they'd been fidgeting with, ballpoint pens. There was a gray-haired man in a short-sleeved plaid shirt, his glasses case held in his breast pocket by a big black flap. Airport faces. Ed had a hard time knowing how to look at them: the young man with the beginnings of a mustache, the salesman with his tie clip, the fat woman in the sleeveless yellow shirt that said *Hussong's Cantina*.

The assistant prosecutor, Larry Cantor, drew in a short sniff of breath, a bald man with sensuous lips and an actor's green eyes. He turned to Ed in his gray suit and said, "You'll sit over there," bowing his head a little in sympathy, one Jewish professional addressing another.

Ed sat down in a chair fronted by what could only be described as an old-fashioned wooden school desk. They told him to face the jurors when he answered the questions, not to face Cantor, who sat to Ed's left with the court reporter, both of them crammed together behind two other similar desks. You had this strange arrangement then of hearing questions from over your left shoulder, but answering them to an audience, who looked at you like an exhibit on a stage. They were only a couple feet away, so close there wasn't even a microphone.

———————

Three hours in the tiny room, with a couple of recesses. The questions were mostly about Great Southwest—the circumstances of its formation, Warren's hidden interest in it, the control he had over James Cornwall. Most of the other questions were about the payments to Talley. No questions about Harry Rosenzweig or Barry Goldwater. Nothing significant about CMS and Chino Grande and Jack Ross, though Ed had described the deal in detail to McCracken and even called it a "fraud." They told him they would like to talk to him again next Tuesday, January 14. Everything he said appeared in summary the next morning in the newspaper under Al Sitter's byline.

———————

I don't think they killed him for what he said, or even for what he might have said later, in further testimony. The initial police theory was that they killed him to deter others from testifying. I think perhaps they killed him simply to show they could do it. They were all planning Phoenix—Warren, the DiFrancos, and the Toccos—all of them with their own motives. In the murder of a witness, their interests happened to coincide. They were going to shake the bush and get the lion to jump out. They were pretty sure the lion didn't exist anyway, and this was a chance to prove it.

Fred Pedote waited in the bushes with the gun in his lap, rain dampening his nylon jacket and the front of his slacks. He'd been drinking and he couldn't sleep and then he drank some more and drove across town to Lazar's house on West San Miguel. It was not just raining but cold, more like Chicago than Phoenix—he didn't think it could be this cold. He was there. It had to do with the use of careful preparation to stop thinking, something like that, or maybe the self-discipline of not feeling drunk when he knew he was drunk.

The only way to leave the house, he thought, was out the front door, then through this courtyard with its cactuses and bougainvillea. The door to the garage was on the courtyard's west side. Pedote wiped his face and closed his eyes against the rain. He would be sitting there as he sat now, on the ground with his legs out in front of him, his back against the wall, looking straight at that door, night turning into day, the cul-de-sac gradually coming alive around him. The straight-laced Jewish accountant, sunlight on his business suit—shoot him right there in the courtyard as he left for work. Stand up out of the bushes, then kneel beside him on the ground and put three more in his chest. That was the photograph: the victim sprawled on his patio, his briefcase tipped over on its side. In the moment it happened, everything would be different in all kinds of small ways, Pedote's heart beating too fast, his mind a jangle of color. He would have to walk very calmly around the side of the house to his car in the back alley. Then he'd have to drive out of there in no hurry, past the garbage cans onto San Miguel.

His hands were numb, but he stayed there for a long time. Maybe it was four o'clock in the morning when he got up, staggering a little in the branches and tearing his foot out of the vines. He walked across the puddles on the tile and unlatched the iron gate. It squeaked a little, as it had when he came in, and then it squeaked again as he latched it behind him. That was when the front door opened and a voice, aiming for deepness, asked who was there.

The iron gate at West San Miguel

He was never afraid. He would joke to Susie sometimes that he would not want to meet Ned Junior in a dark alley, but they never took the jokes seriously. He told the man who sold him life insurance that year that he would not pay the extra few cents a month for a double indemnity clause because it would be a waste of money. "Nothing ever happens to accountants," he said, perhaps a little defiantly. He bought the policy on January 31. He had given his first grand jury testimony on January 9. Nothing had happened to him in twenty-two days. It was the salesman who made the one and only monthly payment—Ed had either forgotten to mail it in or decided he didn't want the policy after all. It didn't cost the salesman much to protect the commission on his new sale.

Ten thousand dollars and no more conversation that Freddy Pedote was selling drugs, that he knew too many people, that he had a mouth and was a risk. Ten thousand dollars after the split with Verive and then Tocco's cut. After he killed Lazar, Freddy was going to keep right on with the coke business anyway, they could all fuck themselves.

From a summary of an interview of John Harvey Adamson conducted by Lonzo McCracken, August 8, 1979:

A short time later Adamson met Pedote in Pedote's apartment. Adamson asked Pedote where he'd been and Pedote said he'd been sick and in St. Joseph's Hospital. Pedote then explained that he had the contract on Lazar and got pneumonia laying in the bushes watching Lazar to determine the best place to kill him. As a result Pedote said that he had to fly someone in to kill Lazar.

20

He wanted everybody killed. That was just all he thought about. They were plotting it just like mafia criminal people, Lee and Kaiser, and that's the way they plot. Someone wanted that contract and they asked someone else and then they brought it to Lee. There was something about this guy, he was doing something to somebody that was affiliated with Dominick DiFranco. He was a real estater. A couple of times Doug and Lee went places and the guy never showed up, he wasn't around there, so Lee—they'd go back by Kaiser's house and Lee would go in and the old lady would go back in the kitchen and then Lee would ask him, what the fuck is this, and then the Old Man would tell him, well I'll find out or I'll go see this guy or see that guy—and they'd exchange names but Doug didn't pay no attention to the names.

Doug was led to believe that the guy in the garage was a killer. That he killed people. That he killed people for Joe Bonanno. And do you know what, it wasn't that way. In the staircase, that guy in the staircase was a fucking coward, okay, but you know what? You can't bring the guy back.

—from the Hardin transcript

Ed washed his hands and looked at himself in the medicine cabinet mirror. A last stop before he left for work, he dried off with a towel and smoothed out his eyebrows. He had an eleven o'clock appointment and a one o'clock appointment, lunch in between with his colleague, Ira Feldman. In the kitchen, in his briefcase, were two tax returns he'd brought home on the pretext of putting in a few hours last night—it was tax season—but he hadn't bothered with them. Instead, he'd played tennis in the evening and relaxed after dinner with Susie and the kids. On the sink in front of him now was a scallop-shaped dish holding five miniature rounds of soap and on the wall beside it hung three decorative towels with a cursive *L* embroidered on them in silk. Things you didn't use but only looked at, sometimes still with the strange recognition that your own house was a kind of mystery, lavender-scented, silent. He liked to make a last bathroom stop before leaving for work, the minute or two alone a time to clear his head and start thinking about the day. He looked once more in the mirror and switched off the light. He wore a gray suit, a blue dress shirt with his initials on the cuffs, a red tie with a small diamond pattern. He wore black high-top mod-style boots, for he was not your average CPA.

He went back out into the kitchen and kissed Susie and the kids good-bye, then he opened the front door and stepped into the courtyard.

Carol Nichols was in her front yard watering a lemon tree when she saw Ed back his car out of the garage, a white-and-maroon Pontiac Grand Ville. She turned to say hello, as she often did, when Ed got out of the idling car to shut the garage door behind him.

"I forgot something," he said. "My breakfast bars." He smiled at Carol in that way that implied so many things: the banality of breakfast bars, his craving for them, the day-to-day thrum of neighborhood life that he relished partly for its innocuous role-playing. He wore a gray suit, a crisp blue shirt, a red tie. He was in a little bit of a hurry, because it was tax season and he had a lot on his mind.

Susie put the breakfast bars in his briefcase on top of the papers, and he took an extra one for the car. She kissed him again and he told her, "You've already done that once." She gave him a playful pinch and told him that she would kiss him anytime she wanted to. Then he went back out to the courtyard. He stepped through the door he had left open and walked through the garage to the driveway, where his car was running, the extra bar in his hand, eating it out of the foil wrapper as he said hello again to Carol Nichols. Then he closed the garage door and got in his car and left, this time for good.

Q: Did Lee kick this guy?
A: Yeah.
Q: Where'd he kick him?
A: In the ass.
Q: Was this after he's dead?
A: After he's down, yeah.
Q: How many times?
A: Actually I thought I walked away and started look-ing around and it seemed like Lee was back there pid-dling with him. But see anytime Lee was around and somebody got shot, Lee always done something to him. Kicked him, drug him, went through his pockets. He'd take the gold out of the teeth, if he had time.

Ed avoided Camelback Road because of the morning traffic and took Bethany Home Road instead. On the radio, the news was oil prices, the recession, a stimulus package in the House, a different one in the Senate. Lloyd Bentsen of Texas had entered the presi-dential race for the Democrats—even in the wake of Watergate, the defeat in Vietnam, the oil crisis, and the recession, the Demo-crats had no one inspiring enough to win so far.

He passed the Chris-Town Mall—the Piccadilly Cafeteria with its tiki-house roofs, Guggy's Coffee Shop, Montgomery Ward and the Broadway and JCPenney, where Susie shopped for the kids. There was Orange Julius and Pizza D'Amore and the Court of Birds, with its vast cages of parrots and parakeets suspended from the ceiling.

Lee DiFranco was thirty-nine years old, short and stout, his hair going white, especially at the sideburns, thinning to a dark frizz on top. He had blue eyes and a straight nose, like the nose on a war mask, a mask of glee. He waited on the second underground level of the parking garage, his partner, Doug Hardin, on the level above it. They waited without anxiety—neither of them drank alcohol or smoked, neither of them was the nervous type. Lee had strangled someone to death three days before in the back of his brother Dominick's Cadillac, a man who was probably named Jack West, whom Lee and Doug called "the Canadian." I have a photograph of Lee DiFranco. I know less about Doug Hardin's appearance. He's in the witness protection program now, if he's still alive. In 1981, Lee DiFranco was beaten to death with a baseball bat and left in the trunk of his Mercedes. Doug Hardin was of medium height and weight with wiry brown hair. I have the 214-page transcript of his scattered recollections of this period, which I had to read three times before it made any sense at all.

———————

Ed turned down North Central Avenue. On the passenger seat was the morning paper, folded over to another headline about the Warren scandal, centered this time on the county prosecutor's investigator, George Brooks. It had been more than a month since Ed had given his grand jury testimony. There had been a series of postponements, but tomorrow he was scheduled to go back for his next session. Last night, he'd received a strange phone call from a man who introduced himself as "Weinstein," a man who claimed to be looking for an accountant for a friend. The call had gotten more and more perplexing and hostile as it went on. Would Ed be in his office tomorrow morning and at what time? Where did he work again? He would be there tomorrow morning? Finally Ed had hung up.

The squeaking gate. The strange phone call. Perhaps there was a reason he'd played tennis yesterday evening instead of looking over the tax returns. Perhaps the reason was that he was trying not to let it get to him.

He crossed Camelback Road and turned left into the parking garage at 3003 North Central Avenue, the First Federal Savings Building. There was a place he liked to park on the second underground level, near Catalina Street, where there were never many cars.

———————

Lee walked over from the stairwell and was standing above him as he opened the door of the Pontiac. He told him to put his briefcase down. He said not to say a fucking word. Then he put the gun to the base of his skull and they walked back toward the stairwell and Lee told him to open the door.

The garage is still there. You can see that my hand was shaking as I took some of the photographs. I parked aboveground on a weekday morning in the middle of rush hour, not much later in the day than he would have arrived. There was sunlight on the level I parked on. I waited outside for an elevator to take me down two floors, holding my camera, feeling conspicuous and morbid while a group of secretaries smiled at me. I was concerned that the garage would not be the same. I was repelled by my desire for it to be the same. At the second underground level, I got out of the elevator alone and started taking the pictures. By now I knew that the garage had not changed in thirty years. At the back corner, off Catalina Street, there were fewer cars. I pushed open the stairwell door and went inside.

It was so small there would have been barely enough room for two people, let alone three. Gray concrete, a filthy fluorescent light bar, like the one that had been unscrewed thirty years ago by Lee DiFranco or Doug Hardin. The stairwell was not wide enough for two people to stand side by side. It was very cold the day I was there, and the narrow space reeked of mildew and dust, as if the door had not been opened in a very long time. I knelt down on the first step—I knew I would do this and now I was doing it almost as a formality. The step was so solid that I felt an immediate pain in my knees and shins. I was shaking. My father would have been shaking, forty years old, a young man, not much older than I was that day. The shape of the stairwell suggested a coffin. It was a tiny cement box in which to be executed. Forty minutes later, the dust was still in my mouth and my nose.

———————

Warren turned white when he heard that Ed was missing. They thought he was having a heart attack. He canceled a business meeting and walked out of the room and went home for the day, and perhaps he wasn't faking. Three people witnessed it and they all tell the story the same way.

He had set up a kind of alibi for himself more than a month before, on the same day my father testified before the grand jury. That evening, Warren had asked Bill Nathan, one of the investors who had bought Consolidated Mortgage, to swear out a complaint against Ed Lazar with the attorney general's office, charging Ed Lazar with fraud. He thought this might neutralize the testimony Ed Lazar had just given that morning. He asked Nathan to tell this to Lonzo McCracken. He also asked Nathan to tell McCracken that he was looking for a deal. He was ill, he had a heart problem, he was afraid he would be convicted and go to jail, he would be completely broke from the legal bills. Perhaps he believed in this version of himself in the moment he presented it to Bill Nathan. Within a year he would be making comments about how Ed Lazar was probably killed by a jealous husband, or because he was selling drugs.

———————

Around nine o'clock that morning, a lawyer named Rad Vukichevich parked in the second underground level of the First Federal Savings Building, where he noticed a Pontiac Grand Ville with its front door open, a briefcase and a set of keys lying on the ground beside it. He informed the parking lot assistant manager, Ruben Lopez, who eventually brought the briefcase and keys to the office of the building manager. Lopez noted the parking permit number on the Pontiac, which could be used to trace its owner. About three hours later, around 1:15, after Ed had missed his eleven and one o'clock and lunch appointments, his office called Susie to ask if she knew where he was. She thought at first that he had just wandered off somewhere, which he did sometimes, often to her annoyance. Around two o'clock, she called the county attorney's office to see if they might have called him in for any further questioning. Around 2:15, three Phoenix police officers were dispatched to the garage and a missing person file was opened. It was about 3:45 when the briefcase and keys finally made it to the office of Harold Toback, Ed's boss, who called Susie again. About seven hours had passed since Lee DiFranco and Doug Hardin had driven off in their station wagon. Detective Wallace Sem discovered the body in the stairwell at 4:47. The Homicide Detail arrived almost two hours later, at 6:40.

It's somewhere around this time that the current span of my memory really begins, in fits and starts, as if some clock in my mind had been reset to zero on that day.

21

On my last night in Phoenix, I met Chuck Kelly, a reporter
for the *Arizona Republic*, at a restaurant in Scottsdale. A few
weeks before, Kelly had done me a great favor by sending me more
than a hundred pages of photocopied news clippings in which my
father's name appeared. Looking through that sheaf of papers, I'd
had the sense of reading a baroquely plotted crime novel com-
posed of found documents, a cacophony of names and faces, facts
and suppositions, and in the silent gaps, as if in some occult code,
the story of what had happened.

Joining us at the bar before we ate was Jon Sellers, a retired
detective from the Phoenix Police Department. He had worked
my father's case for several months in 1975 and 1976. Kelly and
Sellers had known each other for over thirty years, since at least
June of 1976, when one of Kelly's fellow reporters, Don Bolles,
was murdered by a car bomb in the parking lot of the Clarendon
Hotel in downtown Phoenix. The murderer turned out to be
John Adamson—now always referred to as John Harvey Adamson. The most likely scenario is that he'd been hired to do this
by a man named Max Dunlap at the behest of a wealthy Phoenix

businessman named Kemper Marley. The story is byzantine and takes in dozens of names and in some ways it dovetails with the story of my father and Warren. Bolles had been lured to the Clarendon Hotel that afternoon with a tip from Adamson about land fraud, allegedly involving the usual suspects, Barry Goldwater, Congressman Sam Steiger, and Harry Rosenzweig.

Kelly had told me that Sellers was from Texas and a real cowboy, and he was not speaking metaphorically. Sellers stood near the bar in a black fringed jacket and a black wide-brimmed hat, nearing seventy but vigorous and fit. The hostess told him he would have to remove his hat if he wanted to have a seat with us in the dining room and Sellers said no, in that case we would have to talk in the bar.

He asked me, "Where do you want to go?" and I asked him to start with Lonzo McCracken. He said he hadn't trusted McCracken, had always thought McCracken was on a crusade. He was angry that McCracken had not protected my father. I asked if McCracken had offered protection and he said that McCracken claimed he had, but he didn't press hard enough, he should have insisted—a safe house, even overnight stays in jail. What Sellers remembered most about the case had more to do with the physical evidence: my father's briefcase, the ballistics report, what kind of silencer might have been used. He said they'd had a good witness at one point, a woman who said she'd been there in the garage and had heard and seen some things, but that she was scared off by the FBI, who started asking her questions about land fraud.

I told him it seemed obvious to me that Ned Warren had been involved in the murder and Sellers agreed that that was everyone's suspicion. I asked him why Ned Warren had never been so much

Warren died in 1980, having spent the last few years of his life in prison, though mostly out of it on appeal. He had been convicted in federal court along with Gale Nace for the extortion of Dennis Kelly. The Arizona courts had finally convicted him of bribing public officials and of twenty counts of fraud in the sale of Jack Ross's Chino Grande Ranchettes to U.S. servicemen overseas. I spoke to James Cornwall on the telephone just as I was finishing this book. I said I was surprised that he was in Phoenix after all he'd been through, and he told me that his wife's family lived there, it was home, he'd gotten past the point of being intimidated. He had spent three years in Florence Prison looking over his shoulder—three years incarcerated with the very people he had put there with his testimony. They had tried to kill him, as they did kill Tony Serra one day in the prison sign shop. Cornwall said he had had to stop being afraid. He's a retired minister now—in 1984 he founded the Scottsdale Worship Center, an evangelical church. He didn't speak as an evangelist when we talked. I had felt some trepidation about calling him, because I'd already written him into this book—I had never been able to find him before and didn't know he was still alive. I had read about the Rolls-Royce he once owned, the liveried driver, the house in Paradise Valley. I had seen and heard video footage of him from the time period. I had the transcript of a 60 *Minutes* segment in which Cornwall says at one point: "I very kindly throw the responsibility back to the public for falling for such a lousy pitch of nothing more than five hundred free green stamps and a free cowboy lunch, which consisted of a hamburger and some beans." I was cynically unsurprised to find out that Cornwall had become an evangelical preacher. But hearing him talk on the phone, I knew he had earned the authority to believe whatever he believed.

———

Don Bolles is the reason I know so much of this story: my father's yogurt spoons, his dental appointments, his contracts and memos and the restaurants he frequented. When the bomb went off under Don Bolles's car, the windows on one side of the Clarendon Hotel were shattered and guests came out onto their balconies to see a coil of smoke rising into the sky. Bolles himself survived for eleven days of physical agony. They amputated one leg, then the other, then his right arm, in an effort to stop the infection that eventually killed him. His murder led a group of journalists from around the country to join together and descend on Phoenix for six months to investigate what had happened and why. Their effort was called The Arizona Project. The group, the Investigative Reporters and Editors, looked into every dark corner they could find. They published a series of twenty-three articles in several newspapers across the country and accumulated a vast trove of documents and interviews now housed at the University of Missouri in Columbia. I spent days there looking over some of their files and listening to some of their cassettes, and I could have spent several more weeks researching further. In a way, because of those files, I learned more about my father than I might know if he were still alive.

———

As of 2008, they were still sorting out the tangled finances of Cochise College Park, one of Warren's earliest and most compromised projects. Lots had been sold two or three times, mortgages had gone unrecorded, back taxes had accumulated, there were hundreds of owners with contracts and even satisfied mortgages but no titles or deeds. Whole sections of the subdivision were "abandoned to acreage" and sold off at a land auction. One report estimates a total of $40 million in fraud.

I asked around Camp Verde for any information about fraud at Verde Lakes but didn't find anything. The most definitive comment I got there was from a title insurer who told me that by and large Consolidated had a better reputation than Warren's other firms. Later, I found A. A. McCollum, the man who bought Consolidated in 1973 and was tried in federal court for whatever crimes may have been committed before he took over. He and the other three company officers were found innocent.

———————

The Beth El Cemetery is in a small corner of a vast, landscaped compound called the Greenwood Memorial Park on Van Buren Street near the Papago Freeway. A series of small roads leads you from one field to the next, the different sections designated by small numbers painted in white on the trunks of trees. I had never been there before. I drove around and got lost and asked an employee for directions, and eventually I found a small, garage-like building with one wall larger than the others, painted red, a large white stylized menorah in front of it. I had a chart and I had written down the number of my father's plot, which I found after a few more minutes of looking. I ended up staying there much longer than I expected. There was no one else around.

His stone is simple, made of blue-tinted granite, with his name beneath a Star of David, a Hebrew inscription, and the words

Loving Son, Husband & Father. Beneath the dates is another inscription, *Held Close in Our Hearts,* and five more Hebrew letters. His stone is next to my grandparents' stone, Louis and Belle Lazar, who both survived their son by ten years. They are buried side by side and share a stone that says *Lazar* and gives their names and dates beneath.

There are rituals but I don't know them. The grayish blue stones sat amid the dead grass, which was yellow and dry as hay. I brushed them clean of some clippings left there by a lawn mower. I didn't know when the last time was that anyone had come to these graves and I understood in a way I never had before why such visits are necessary. I looked at the gray stone and imagined the forty-year-old man. Silence, the three of them there—my father and my grandparents—the highway nearby, so close you could see the cars in their crowded lanes. It was a sunny day, the blue sky very still, cloudless and cold.

People talk about the mystery of evil, but evil seems less mysterious to me than good. The word *good* is harder to say with conviction than the word *evil—good* is harder to define. In the Jewish tradition, you can't call it by name. It's called *Adonai*. To say the actual word would be to denigrate its mystery, which is not only gentle but fierce, perhaps even inclusive of evil. When Job asked God why God had forsaken him, this is the knowledge I think Job received.

He came alive for me while I wrote this book. I still can't remember him, but I will remember this portrait of him. A kind of conjuration. Another stone to mark his passage on this earth.

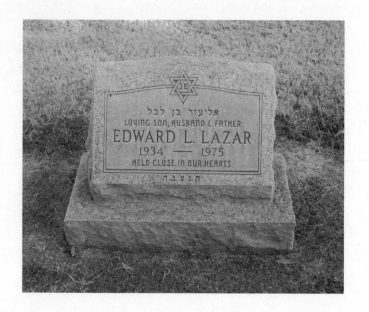

ACKNOWLEDGMENTS

In 2006, I started researching this book with a phone call to a Phoenix police sergeant named Mike Torres, whose name appeared in the *Arizona Republic* article that now opens the prologue. Torres and I talked about my project and he gave me several leads, including the obvious but very valuable recommendation to call Chuck Kelly, one of the two reporters who had written the article. Immediately, Chuck made this project viable—on his own time, he went through the *Republic*'s archives and sent me copies of every article they'd printed that included my father's name. In addition, he shared with me his extensive knowledge of Arizona in the time period. Another reporter, since deceased, Al Sitter, also gave to me of his time and memories. Kelly's and Sitter's articles and those written by their colleagues at the *Republic* and the *Phoenix Gazette* provided me with much of the factual outline of this book. I also referred constantly to the work of The Arizona Project reporters, and to Michael F. Wendland's account of their story in his book, *The Arizona Project*. In an era when the very survival of print journalism is in jeopardy, the work of these writers is a vivid reminder of the importance of newspapers, and I thank them for what they've done. Thanks also to Dave Wagner, an expert on this period in Arizona's history and its staggering array of figures.

Through their recollections, my father's friends and family members gave me the ability to imagine him beyond the bare sketch provided by my documentary research. I owe an enormous debt of gratitude to Carol Nichols Turoff, Ted and Elaine Kort, Ron Fineberg, Beverly Fineberg, Murray Goodman, Harry Swirnoff, Earl Geller, Ira Feldman, Norton Stillman, and Jeff Lazar. Thanks also to David Nichols. Above all, thanks to my mother, who supported this book from the beginning and, so that I could write it, relived some of her most painful memories.

I want to also thank George Weisz, senior assistant to the mayor of Phoenix; former Phoenix police detective Jon Sellers; Linda Whitaker of the Arizona Historical Foundation; William Stolz and David F. Moore at the Western Historical Manuscript Collection at the University of Missouri; Beth Kopine and Mark Horvit at Investigative Reporters and Editors; Ron Passarelli and Vicky Rokkos at the Arizona Department of Real Estate; Tim Muse of Land Am Title; Tina McMillian at the Arizona attorney general's office; former Maricopa County prosecutor Don Harris; Bill Farrow; A. A. McCollum; Dave Cross; James Cornwall; Winojene Harris; Tom Henze; and Chris Nolan.

My agent, Bill Clegg, and my editor, Pat Strachan, both gave me enormous encouragement and help with *Evening's Empire*, for which I am deeply grateful. I owe a special thanks to Pat for getting this book over the many unforeseen obstacles that emerged throughout the process. Thanks to everyone at Little, Brown: Vanessa Kehren, Marlena Bittner, Katherine Molina, Terry Adams, Allison Warner, Pamela Marshall, and Michael Pietsch.

Finally, many sincere thanks to my family—all Lazars, Lackners, Watsons, Cottrells, and Patins.

ABOUT THE AUTHOR

Zachary Lazar has received a Guggenheim Fellowship and holds a 2009–2010 Hodder Fellowship at Princeton University. *Evening's Empire* is his third book.

Reading Group Guide

EVENING'S EMPIRE

THE STORY OF MY FATHER'S MURDER

by

ZACHARY LAZAR

AFTER *EVENING'S EMPIRE*

At all times, the most unlikely situations are unfolding all around us.

The week after *Evening's Empire* was published a critic singled out this particular sentence as "feeble padding," but the review itself led to yet another unlikely situation.

It was seen by a woman in South Hadley, Massachusetts, who had been wondering about me for a long time, for almost two decades. She tracked down an e-mail address for me and wrote a brief note. I didn't know whether to believe what she had to say at first, so we corresponded some more and finally I asked the woman—her name is Amy Brady—to send me a photograph of herself. It turns out that she is my half sister.

In 1963, Amy's biological mother was living in Phoenix, where she dated a Jewish accountant named Ed Lazar and became pregnant. She told him that she was putting the baby up for adoption. Amy, the baby, was taken in by a Jewish couple in Roslyn, New York, about an hour from where I now live. Her biological mother went back to Oklahoma and they had no contact until the 1990s, when the mother found her. They met and started a relationship. Eventually the biological mother told Amy that on a trip to Phoenix in the early seventies she had run into her former boyfriend, Ed Lazar, Amy's father. They hadn't seen each other for more than ten years. He told her he was married now, that he and his wife had two children. Not long after this chance meeting she learned that Ed Lazar had been murdered.

It was unlikely that she would have run into him in Phoenix, but she did. During this chance meeting, he didn't mention the names of his wife or children. What Amy knew for almost two decades was that she had two half siblings out there—she had grown up an only child—but that was all she knew and all she was able to find out.

In January 2010, about two months after she read the book review that prompted her to contact me, Amy came back to Roslyn, where I drove to meet her for the first time. I felt comfortable with her by then—we had talked on the phone—but I had just returned from a book tour that brought back some anxieties. On the tour, among other things, I had met Ned Warren's granddaughter, who, for reasons I still don't understand, had come to a talk I gave at the Arizona Attorney General's Office, a talk during which her grandfather was repeatedly named as the man who'd ordered my father's murder. I found myself looking out of the corner of my eye throughout my stay in Phoenix. I knew there was no practical reason for Amy to pretend to be my half sister, but I was still in a slightly paranoid frame of mind when I went to meet her that afternoon in Roslyn.

We had lunch at a French bistro near the duck pond in the center of town. Amy is a physical trainer and a vegan, and ever since our first conversation I have found her interesting and pleasant to talk with. We are both addicted to running. She told me the story of her childhood and adolescence in Roslyn, an affluent town where she sometimes felt out of place. After lunch, we went for a drive in her car to the beach. I had a flash of paranoia—this was all a complicated setup that would end with some accomplice from Chicago in the empty parking lot breaking my legs—but the flash subsided and we went for a walk on the freezing January boardwalk.

I was about to interview that February for a visiting writer job at Amherst College. Amherst is just a few miles from Amy's house in South Hadley. It was in South Hadley that we met for the second time, and where I met Amy's adoptive mother and her sixteen-year-old son, Nicholas. I realized that if I got the job, I would be spending the next three years there.

Unlikely situations unfolding all around us.

Two years before, independent of any of this, an English teacher at Roslyn High School—Amy's alma mater—happened to read a review of another book of mine, called *Sway*. He not only read and liked the book, but he decided to add it to his syllabus. Shortly after my first meeting with Amy, he wrote to invite me to visit his class. He had never met Amy or heard of her. I asked him if she could come, and when he said yes, she drove down from Massachusetts with Nicholas. Like me at fifteen, Nicholas is passionate about playing guitar, writing songs, reading, and writing fiction. He goes to a prep school in Northampton called Williston, the same prep school my father-in-law went to.

If I hadn't written *Evening's Empire*, I wouldn't know any of this. After the visit to Amy's old school, we went back to the restaurant near the duck pond. It was June this time and we used our cell phones to take pictures of ourselves on a bench outside. It is strange to meet a sibling with whom you have no shared past. Perhaps the most unlikely situation is not meeting Amy but our having anything in common. We left that afternoon with plans to see each other again in a few months.

I should say that there was more to my Phoenix trip than paranoia. With my mother and my sister Stacey, I went to a party hosted by some of my parents' old friends, Ted and Elaine Kort. I don't think anyone knew what to expect. Many of the people there had not seen each other in years. I was relieved to find that they liked the book, that they felt I had got my father's character down on the page with a vividness that surprised them (my mother also thought this). But, more important, the party was an occasion for people to talk about what had happened all those years ago, about the man they'd known and how much they'd loved him. It became a kind of accidental memorial. Later, I went to Minneapolis, my father's hometown, and met more of his friends, heard more of their stories, and had this same feeling of commemoration. If I hadn't written this book, none of these unlikely situations would have unfolded.

A CONVERSATION WITH ZACHARY LAZAR

How did your family react to Evening's Empire?

My family was very supportive. I was concerned about my mother in particular and we talked many times, even before I started working on the book, trying to decide whether or not I should write it.

We talked throughout the research—sometimes what I was finding out about my father would look flattering, sometimes not; sometimes the qualities of the same piece of information would change entirely in the light of something new. Talking about this, of course, meant that we also had to talk about the past in a much more comprehensive way than we had before—my parents' whole lives together and finally my father's death. It was the most difficult part of the book for me by far. When my mother read it, I was relieved to hear that she approved.

The book combines various kinds of writing—journalism, memoir, even fiction. Why did you construct the book this way?

I knew that, as important as my father's story was to me personally, I also had to make it important to an audience of strangers. I had to use whatever tools I had—not as an ideal teller of the tale, but as me, a novelist.

There was a factual story to be told: What were the events that led up to the murder? Who was involved? How did it happen? Then there was a bigger mystery to consider: Why are people murdered at all? Which is to ask: What is evil? And so it seemed that the facts alone were not going to be quite enough.

To make the facts live as I wanted them to live—for me to understand them in the way I wanted to understand them—meant that I would have to try to imagine them playing out. Because how can you have even an inkling of what evil is, or is like, if you never get beyond the rational? And how can evil register for the writer or for the reader if it is not evoked and made emotional?

Was writing this book about your father's murder cathartic?

Others have asked that question, and I find myself uncomfortable with the word "cathartic." I believe in catharsis, but I think of it as a fleeting, delicate state of mind, like joy or sadness.

If it is indeed fleeting, then catharsis is actually the opposite of closure, that other word we hear so much in connection with loss or grief. Closure implies a wrapping-up of affairs. I've never understood how this is any different from forgetting or just not thinking or feeling.

It is in fact by opening up—by confronting what is otherwise too difficult or unpleasant to think about—that we achieve catharsis. There are a lot of casualties by the time we get to the end of *King Lear.* Our pleasure in *The Tempest* is that we've seen how much could have gone wrong but didn't. A play or a book can probably not change us very much in any permanent way, but catharsis is important in the same way that joy and sadness are important. Catharsis lets us feel a kind of dignity that we are frequently unable to feel.

QUESTIONS AND TOPICS FOR DISCUSSION

1. Have you ever discovered something about your parents that made you think of them differently? How did you respond emotionally to this discovery?

2. Discuss the various identities of Ned Warren, Sr.: N. J. Warren, Ned, Nathan Jacques Warren, Nathan Jacques Waxman. How did Warren use these names to create different personas? What was your impression of Warren?

3. *Evening's Empire* is a story about American ambition and idealism. Zachary Lazar writes: "What [Ed Lazar] wanted was to not feel invisible, to not feel like he was failing just because he didn't want or have the boat, the second house, the better car" (page 48). What do you think the author means by "to not feel invisible"? How is this different from accumulating wealth?

4. Ned Warren's charismatic personality was seductive to many people, including Ed Lazar. Is it possible that it blinded Lazar to the reality of Warren's business? Have you ever been swept up in something only to discover later that you had made a mistake? Were you able to remove yourself from the situation? How?

5. Do you think the mortgage scams described in *Evening's Empire* bear any resemblance to the current subprime mortgage crisis that led to turmoil in the financial sector? Why or why not?

6. In researching and writing this book, part of Zachary Lazar's goal was to untangle his father's level of involvement in Ned Warren's business practices and discover the extent of his knowledge of their illegal activities. Do you think that the people who worked for Warren should have been held responsible even if they weren't aware of the extent of the fraud?

7. Do you know the Bob Dylan song "Mr. Tambourine Man," which inspired the title of *Evening's Empire*? If so, how do you think the tone of the book reflects the mood of Dylan's lyrics and music?

8. "At all times, the most unlikely situations are unfolding all around us. It is our own luck that allows us not to see it. Our luck allows us not to see the people in the shadows, or not to see them as they really are. It is the people in the shadows who see us as we really are" (page 51). Discuss how this passage relates to the book. Do you agree with it?

9. No one was ever tried or convicted of Edward Lazar's murder, and his case was cleared in 1995. What do you think were the reasons for the apparent cover-up? How would you respond if a severely wronged loved one did not receive justice?

10. Zachary Lazar calls his portrait of his father a "conjuration." Although he does not remember much about him, he uses fictional techniques, among other tools, to re-create a man he might like to have known. Do you think the author is justified in using the literary conventions of fiction to bring his father back to life? Why or why not?

11. How does *Evening's Empire* reflect what you know as the Wild West? Did this contemporary account of the lawlessness in the American West take you by surprise?

Also by Zachary Lazar
SWAY

"A brilliant novel... elegant and intricate.... *Sway* reads like your parents' nightmare idea of what would happen to you if you fell under the spell of rock 'n' roll."
— Charles Taylor, *New York Times Book Review*

"Blending fact and myth, Lazar casts the Rolling Stones, the Manson family, and avant-garde filmmaker Kenneth Anger as characters in his dizzying, foreboding shadow history of the sixties."
— *Rolling Stone*

"Compelling.... One succumbs to this richly imagined, hauntingly vivid novel, wherein everyone falls under the sway of someone or something." — Gregory Leon Miller, *San Francisco Chronicle*

"Lazar has created a powerful, infernal prism through which to view the potent, still-rippling contradictions of the late sixties. It's no mean feat." — Mark Rozzo, *Los Angeles Times Book Review*

"Hypnotic.... It is not the now-historic acts of violence that make *Sway* so riveting, but its vivid character portraits and decadent, muzzy atmosphere, all rendered with the heightened sensory awareness associated with drugs and paranoia."
— Liz Brown, *Time Out New York*

"A rare find, both violent and beautiful." — *GQ*

Back Bay Books
Available wherever paperbacks are sold